Of Human
Potential

Of Human Potential

An Essay in the Philosophy of Education

Israel Scheffler

ROUTLEDGE & KEGAN PAUL

Boston, London, Melbourne and Henley

First published in 1985
by Routledge & Kegan Paul plc

9 Park Street, Boston, Mass. 02108, USA

14 Leicester Square, London WC2H 7PH, England

464 St Kilda Road, Melbourne,
Victoria 3004, Australia and

Broadway House, Newtown Road,
Henley on Thames, Oxon RG9 1EN, England

Set in Linotron Times, 10 on 12 pt
by Input Typesetting Ltd, London
and printed in Great Britain
by St Edmundsbury Press
Bury St Edmunds, Suffolk

Library of Congress Cataloging in Publication Data

Scheffler, Israel.
Of human potential.
Bibliography: p.
Includes index.
1. Education – Philosophy. 2. Education and state. 3. Educational
anthropology. 4. Intellect. I. Title.
LA132.S328   1985   370'.1   85–2140

British Library CIP data also available

ISBN 0–7102–0571–6

For Adam Nathaniel Scheffler

CONTENTS

Contents

NOTE ON THE PROJECT ON
HUMAN POTENTIAL

The Bernard van Leer Foundation of The Hague, Netherlands is an international non-profit making institution dedicated to the cause of disadvantaged children and youth. It supports innovative projects that develop community approaches to early childhood education and child care, in order to help disadvantaged children to realize their potential.

In 1979, the Foundation asked the Harvard Graduate School of Education to assess the state of scientific knowledge concerning human potential and its realization. Proceeding from this general directive, a group of scholars at Harvard has over the past several years been engaged in research exploring the nature and realization of human potential. Activities sponsored by the Project on Human Potential have included reviews of relevant literature in history, philosophy and the natural and social sciences, a series of international workshops on conceptions of human development in diverse cultural traditions, and the commissioning of papers and books.

The principal investigators of the Project represent a variety of fields and interests. Gerald S. Lesser, who chaired the Project's steering committee, is an educator and developmental psychologist, a principal architect in the creation of educational television programs for children. Howard Gardner is a psychologist who has studied the development of symbolic skills in normal and gifted children, and the impairment of such skills in brain-damaged adults. Israel Scheffler is a philosopher who has worked in the areas of philosophy of education, philosophy of science, and philosophy of language. Robert LeVine, a social anthropologist, has worked in subsaharan Africa and Mexico, studying family life, child care and psychological development. Merry White is a sociologist and Japan specialist who has studied education, formal organizations and the roles of women in the Third World and Japan. This wide range of interests and disciplines enabled the Project to take a multi-faceted approach to issues of human potential.

The first volume published under the aegis of the Project was Howard Gardner's *Frames of Mind* (Basic Books, 1983), a study of human intellectual potentials which drew not only on psychological research but also on the biological sciences and on findings about the development and use of knowledge in different cultures.

The present volume is the second book of the Project to appear, and it offers a treatment of philosophical aspects of the concept of potential. Sketching the background of the concept and placing it in the context of a general theory of human nature, this treatment then proposes three analytical reconstructions of the concept and offers systematic reflections on policy and the education of policy-makers.

The third volume to appear will be *Human Conditions: The Cultural Basis of Educational Development*, by Robert A. LeVine and Merry I. White. Emphasizing the crucial role of cultural factors in the progress of human development, the book offers new models for development based on the social anthropology of the lifespan and the social history of family and school.

To provide background for the study of diversity in development, the Project established teams of consultants in Egypt, India, Japan, Mexico, the People's Republic of China and West Africa. Selected papers presented by these consultants in Project workshops will appear in a fourth volume, to appear under the editorship of Merry I. White and Susan Pollak. Representatives of international development agencies were also engaged as consultants and correspondents over the five-year period of the Project. Through such international dialogue and research, the Project has sought to create a new multidisciplinary environment for understanding human potential.

PREFACE

This book offers an interpretation of the concept of human potential, which plays a prominent role in the thinking of parents, educators, and planners the world over. Although this concept accurately reflects central features of human nature, its current use perpetuates traditional myths of fixity, harmony and value calculated to cause untold mischief in social and educational practice. My aim in this book is to show the roots of the concept of potential in genuine aspects of human nature while at the same time freeing it, through analytical reconstruction, of outworn philosophical myths. I hope thereby to improve both its theoretical and its practical applicability.

The genesis of the book in the Project on Human Potential is explained in the note on pages ix–x and further elaborated in my Introduction. I want here, however, to express my warm thanks to the Bernard van Leer Foundation, which conceived and sponsored the Project and, in particular, to William Welling and Oscar van Leer, as well as their associates at the Foundation.

I am indebted to my senior colleagues on the Project – Howard Gardner, Gerald Lesser, Robert LeVine and Merry White – for the invaluable contributions they have made to my continuing education on topics of Project interest, as well as for their skeptical and spirited responses to ideas of my own. The work I present here is an outcome of genuinely critical and constructive collaboration.

Research assistants in the Project have been indispensable to its progress and completion. I have benefited from all, but I must thank, in particular, Susan McConnell, whose instruction on

xi

neurobiological topics was enormously helpful to me; Susan Pollak, who explored relevant aspects of the history of ideas; Elizabeth Fine, who offered valuable assistance with library research; and Kenneth Hawes, who provided close critical readings of my manuscript during the final year of the Project. Other Project associates who helped in various ways included Margaret Herzig, Harry Lasker and Linda Levine. Dean Paul N. Ylvisaker was one of the initial architects of the Project; both he and his successor, Dean Patricia Graham, provided steadfast support.

Several philosophical colleagues who were not members of the Project read the entire manuscript and provided me with extensive comments; to Professors Harry S. Broudy, Thomas F. Green and Jonas Soltis I am grateful for their helpful criticisms and advice. The manuscript was also read and discussed at a seminar of the Philosophy of Education Research Center at Harvard, and I thank my seminar colleagues – Catherine Z. Elgin, Vernon A. Howard, Kenneth Hawes and David N. Perkins – for their critical observations and suggestions. I must, finally, mention the secretarial help afforded me throughout by Shirley Foster, and the typing and word processing assistance of Dolly Appel of the Project, who prepared the manuscript meticulously, diligently and with friendly good cheer.

ACKNOWLEDGMENTS

The author and publishers are grateful for permission to reproduce copyright material, as follows: to Harvard University Press for D. N. Perkins, *The Mind's Best Work* (1981) and Ralph Barton Perry, *Realms of Value* (1954); to the North-Holland Publishing Co. for W. D. Wall, 'Research and the Bernard van Leer Foundation' from the *International Journal of Behavioral Development*, vol. 1 (1978); to David Perkins for the paper 'Constructive Learning' (1984); to the Social Science Research Council for Francis X. Sutton, 'Rationality, Development and Scholarship' from *Items*, vol. 36, no. 4 (1982); to the University of Chicago Press for F. A. Olafson, *The Dialectic of Action* (1979); to the World Bank for Everett M. Rogers, Nat J. Colletta and Joseph Mbindyo, 'Social and Cultural Influences on Human Development Policies and Programs' from the World Bank Staff Working Paper no. 403, 'Implementing Programs of Human Development' (1980).

INTRODUCTION: TOWARD A PRACTICAL THEORY

This book is an essay in the philosophy of education, dealing primarily with the concept of potential. Starting with an account of human nature purporting to show the practical motivation of this concept, the book proceeds to reconstruct it analytically, and to indicate how the analysis applies to selected empirical materials. The book then concludes with an interpretation of policy-making in education, reflecting on the ideal education of a policy-maker. Throughout the several chapters, there is an emphasis on human symbolism, choice, temporal continuity and self-determination, aspects I take to be indispensable for any adequate philosophy of education.

The book owes its existence to my participation in the Harvard Project on Human Potential, reporting investigations I undertook as a Project member. Some remarks on the background and purpose of this enterprise may thus be of interest. The Project was established at the Harvard Graduate School of Education in 1979, with a grant from the Bernard van Leer Foundation of The Netherlands. The Foundation, to quote from a self-description in its *Newsletter*, 'promotes innovative models in education related to socially deprived children and young people. It supports projects which enable the young to benefit as fully as possible from their educational and social development opportunities; and thereby, to fulfil their own potential and to make their maximum contribution to the advancement of society.'[1] A recent report of the Board of Trustees declares the mission of the Foundation to

1

be 'the realization of potential among disadvantaged and deprived groups.'[2]

The centrality of *potential* in Foundation thinking is representative of the prominent role of this concept in the thought of teachers, parents and planners generally. Such centrality explains the original purpose behind the Harvard project: the Foundation sought illumination of its fundamental aims and guidance in conceiving its basic activities. What it asked of the Harvard project group was the development of a theoretical framework for conceiving human potential that would be both analytically sound and scientifically informed, the assumption being that, aside from its intrinsic interest, such a framework would be practically valuable for the guidance of education. This is the substantial challenge which the Project on Human Potential undertook to meet.

Not without considerable misgivings, however. For the notion of potential, though it figures heavily in writings on education and development, is neither a theoretical term of the contemporary human sciences nor a focus of current philosophical analysis; it has, moreover, both traditional and popular connotations which would, in any event, need to be avoided. An attempt to produce a scientific 'theory' of potential from scratch would thus seem quixotic in the extreme if, indeed, it were not simply to mask a trivial translation of familiar stuff into the idiom of potential. On the other hand, without the attempt to produce a theory of potential from scratch, what would acceptance of the Foundation's challenge amount to? Would it entail a synthesis of all that is known about human nature and culture, all that has been said and thought about learning and teaching? What limits were to be set? The challenge seemed, in short, to require either a false specificity or a rudderless generality.

To define the problem so as to avoid these twin evils was the Project's first – and continuing – order of business. We have striven throughout to organize our efforts so that, without presupposing a self-evident role in scientific theory for the concept of potential, we could yet hope, through science and philosophy, to illuminate its currency in contexts of education and development, thereby improving our general understanding of these contexts. For what was clear to us from the first – and became increasingly salient as our work proceeded – was that the notion of potential fulfills significant functions in educational decision-making, at the critical junctures of past and future, fact and value. To identify and analyze such functions seemed to us to promise new insights into educational practice, and to point the way to improved norms by which such practice might be guided.

How, in particular, was the analysis to proceed? The point was not simply to codify or elaborate the scientifically established uses of the concept of potential, for there are none such. Since no discipline in the human sciences in fact couches its content in the idiom of potential, the analysis could not be conceived as the appendage of any given discipline. But neither could the general ideal of multidisciplinary synthesis offer sufficient guidance: which disciplines were to be synthesized, how exactly were they to be joined, and to what purpose? The analysis certainly required greater breadth than any single discipline would allow, but also sufficient limitation so that it could be carried out in a structured fashion.

That the language of potential finds its natural home not in current social science but rather in educational practice provided us with an important focus and a strategy of study. We could try, in the spirit of philosophical analysis, to scrutinize such language against the background of educational purposes and decisions, to investigate its origins, functions and cogency as a tool of practical thought, and to reconstruct it where necessary and desirable. Since assertions and denials of educational potential in practice typically invoke the authority of psychology and the social sciences, we could, further, try to see what bearing these empirical studies have on such practical claims, both as ordinarily understood, and as philosophically reinterpreted.

Within psychology, we took development studies as our special point of departure since claims of potential and rebuttals thereof frequently rest on views of human development. However, we understood such development as theoretically the joint concern of increasingly integrated biological and psychological inquiries. Within the social sciences, our focus was primarily anthropological, not only because of the obvious fact that individual development takes place always within a particular culture, and not alone because educational decision-making often makes assumptions as to the developmental potential of whole groups and even societies. In addition, we wanted to guard, as far as possible, against cultural bias in the attempt to deal scientifically with basic

3

questions of human nature. Thus, we sought to build cross-cultural dialogue into our inquiries from the very first, giving voice to the wide variety characterizing beliefs of different cultures as to human development. Through studies of a number of non-Western countries, conducted collaboratively with scholars of those countries, the Project tried to document a range of conceptions regarding education, thus allowing for more realistic generalization of our studies than would otherwise be possible.

As the relatively independent philosophical, psychological, and anthropological strands of Project inquiries developed, we strove to weave them ever more closely together. Through philosophical analysis of the language of potential and its practical functions, we hoped to identify those features of mind and culture especially relevant to educational endeavor. Conversely, through progressing psychological and anthropological studies, we sought to determine those human characteristics of central importance for philosophical interpretation. Similarly, the individual focus of the psychologist and the cultural focus of the anthropologist increasingly informed one another as our studies proceeded. And the effort to hold practical contexts of education in view helped further to integrate the perspectives of our disciplines and to relate them to considerations of value and decision.

The Harvard Project, in sum, took as its purpose to provide an analysis of potential pertinent to educational practice, and to use such analysis in organizing empirical knowledge relevant to such practice. The results of our work are reported in full in four volumes, of which the present book, detailing the philosophical and conceptual aspects of our inquiry, is the second to appear. Howard Gardner's *Frames of Mind*[3] has already presented the psychological aspects and a third volume, by Merry I. White and Robert LeVine, will deal with anthropological matters. A fourth volume presents accounts of Project studies of non-Western countries, mentioned earlier.

The foregoing discussion describes what the Project tried to do. Whether it in fact succeeded in producing an illuminating account is for others to judge. But one point is important to note if such judgment is to be fair to our intent, and that point concerns the concept of *theory*. We did not, as emphasized earlier, attempt to construct a scientific theory of potential nor to report on some mythical science of potential, already available. In what sense was our work theoretical at all, then? Briefly, the answer is that we hoped to develop, not a scientific theory, but a practical theory.

A scientific theory is a law-like statement or set of statements, formulated in the vocabulary of a scientific discipline, which claims to give a truthful representation of the phenomena studied by the discipline. A scientific theory is judged by its contribution to the understanding of such phenomena; in practice, it is assessed by its logical coherence, its explanatory power, and its heuristic fruitfulness, as judged by the methodological canons of the discipline. Science tends toward increasing systematization of theory and progressive abstractness of vocabulary. In its drive toward ever more comprehensive explanation, its theories comprise increasingly autonomous and integrated structures, with constituent terms departing further and further from the familiar language of everyday practical experience. The organization of theoretical knowledge within a scientific discipline is, in short, dictated by the twin aims of general understanding and the further growth of such understanding.

A practical theory, by contrast, organizes its propositions so as to provide guidance to some practical enterprise, for example, the healing of the sick, the construction of shelters, the rearing of the young. In the professions associated with these enterprises, namely, medicine, engineering, and education, we have primary examples of such differing organization. The knowledge relevant to any one of these professions is drawn from no single scientific discipline. A variety of disciplines, rather, must be presupposed in typical professional work, the practical problems addressed being unconstrained by the limits of any single one and spilling over into each.

Moreover, beyond every disciplinary account available, there are elements of knowledge and value that enter into all professional activity. There is, first of all, knowledge of an array of problems as they present themselves in relevant contexts of practice rather than contexts of inquiry. The patient feels pain or cannot walk; the bridge sways or is too narrow to accommodate rush-hour traffic; the child is having difficulty reading. Each of these descriptions is couched, not in the specialized language of a discipline, but in the idiom of everyday life. Each expresses, not a law-like generalization, but the character of a situation affecting human beings who are disposed to notice and respond to it in one

5

way or another, even if not by overt action. Such expressions, in whatever language is natural to the persons in question, are essential to identifying the problems which professions must treat. They form part of the practical theory underlying a profession.

Second, professions are governed by distinctive purposes defining their scope and limits. The basic knowledge of the physician can be used to poison as well as to heal, but the ethics of medicine is not neutral on this question, forbidding the one and enjoining the other. A profession embodies comprehensive values respecting the problematic choices falling within its purview. Statements of such values and associated principles of action are indispensable constituents of its practical theory.

The organization of a practical theory is dictated, not by the aim of advancing general understanding, but by the effort to guide decision in some realm of practice. It is the practical questions of such a realm which provide the common focus for the elements of its practical theory. From a purely disciplinary point of view, such a theory is composite, inelegant, roughly hewn. But for the purpose it is meant to serve in guiding practical judgment, a composite account is clearly more functional than a purely disciplinary theory would be. Who would choose to ride over a bridge whose builder knew only theoretical physics but nothing about the stresses of available materials or the local functions to be served by the bridge? Who would elect a surgeon who knew only biochemistry, or only physiology, or only anatomy but nothing about other relevant disciplines or the patient's history or the success rate of the surgical procedure in question? Aside from the clinical training and experience of the aspiring professional, his theoretical education must surely be understood as composite if it is to be effective. For it is the task of the professional to draw together the understandings achieved by relevant disciplines and to apply them, under the guidance of an ethical ideal, to the problems of ordinary experience.[4]

Which disciplines are to be included in a given professional curriculum, what weight each is to be given, and how they are to be integrated in practical training are difficult questions requiring continuous attention and admitting of no solutions by formula. But that some multiplicity is required in any case is not to be doubted. Now the Harvard Project can be interpreted as contributing to a practical theory of educational decision-making, incorpo-

6

rating several disciplinary perspectives, an ethical point of view, and a conceptual scheme helping to relate these elements to one another and point them toward practice. The work of the Project is, in sum, an implicit attempt to specify how a curriculum for the preparation of educational decision-makers might be conceived.

The present book outlines philosophical aspects of the Project's work. The order of topics to be pursued is as follows: Chapter I presents fundamental conceptions of human nature and value that serve as a basis both for the ensuing analysis of potential and the later discussion of policy. The chapter first addresses the functions of references to potential in educational practice. These functions are held to take their rise in special features of human nature, which are then characterized in the main portion of the chapter. Three myths of potential are identified and criticized, in passing. The ensuing account of human nature emphasizes the capacity for choice by active beings who symbolically represent both their environments and their options, imagining futures and recollecting pasts, forging durable selves and communities structured by ideals and rules, and creating, above the biological substrate of their lives, the realm of human history.

The centrality of intention and choice in the foregoing account requires reference to value, and we are indeed concerned to study the evaluative connotations of the language of potential. Our very study, itself guided by intention and choice, thus also exemplifies values and cannot, in this respect, pretend to be value-free. Accordingly, we attempt, in the final part of Chapter I, to characterize our normative suppositions and to spell out their ramifications.

Having laid the groundwork in the foregoing discussions, we proceed in Chapter II to a consideration of received notions of potential, bearing in mind the roles ordinarily played by such notions in practice. We are particularly concerned with inherited doctrines of essence and natural kinds, which exercise a lingering influence. Critical of such doctrines, we proceed next to offer three reconstructions of the language of potential which, as we argue, together provide a sounder basis than traditional notions for understanding its practical uses. These reconstructions constitute our conceptual framework for potential.

Chapter III outlines selected empirical applications of this conceptual framework. The purpose of the chapter is to illustrate how the analytical notions earlier presented may be employed to describe salient features of the phenomena. We attempt to show the applicability of our framework at four levels, the biological, the psychological, the cross-cultural and the educational, thus facilitating not only the interpretation but also the integration of materials drawn from these four levels. A coda to the chapter outlines some practical effects of a demythologized notion of potential.

Finally, in Chapter IV, we explore the import of our earlier discussions for educational policy and for the education of policy makers. What broad conceptions implicit in our view of human nature as well as in our analytic notions and their applications bear significantly on the realm of educational policy and the process of decision-making? This is the question to which our concluding chapter is addressed, and it serves to take us from considerations of conceptual analysis and empirical findings to reflections on policy and practice in education. Which, in view of the whole structure and point of our study, is as it should be.

This book is a *philosophical* effort. Some remarks may be welcome here to clarify the nature and point of such an effort. Why, it may be asked, develop a philosophical analysis of the concept of potential when we are sufficiently clear as to how to deploy it in practice? And what does such analysis amount to anyhow?

Now it is true that in everyday life, we discourse freely not only about what things are but about what they might possibly be, not only about what people do but about what they can or might or are likely to do, not only about actual or manifest characteristics, but also about potential characteristics. In familiar contexts and for ordinary practical purposes, it is indeed often adequately clear what is meant by such discourse, even though there may be disagreements over its application to particular cases.

When, however, such discourse is put to theoretical use in science or philosophy, or applied in weighty or novel circumstances of practice, a higher level of clarity and explicitness is required: what definitions of possibility are presupposed; what are the relevant criteria of likelihood; under what conditions is it to be said that someone *might* do something; what evidence is required for judging what a thing can do as distinct from what it actually does, or holding a characteristic to be potential though not manifest? Such questions are not easily put to rest by reliance on familiar or traditional conceptions. We need rather to attempt a formulation of basic principles in a clear, general and precise manner, that is to say, in a philosophical spirit.

Perfect precision and absolute clarity are, to be sure, will o' the wisps. No effort at elucidation can proceed without assumptions. The very process of clarifying certain concepts requires us to take others for granted meanwhile, and to assume throughout a method of clarification. However, it does not follow from these consider-ations that clarification is impossible.

At any given time, we each of us find certain concepts more comprehensible than others, certain methods more cogent than their rivals. Assuming these concepts and methods for the time being, we effect our theoretical clarifications relative to them. Finding cause at a later time to question our earlier procedure or conclusions, we repeat the process under revised assumptions. The elucidatory process is continuous and relative throughout, but clarification is none the less recognizably achieved. We require only to be forthright in acknowledging our assumptions at each point, understanding that other assumptions may appeal to different theorists.

Concepts belong to families. The family with which the concept of potentiality is affiliated, including possibility, capacity, power, tendency, likelihood, and still others, has been the focus of intense philosophical interest and the subject of philosophical controversy from ancient times to the present. Our aim in the present book is decidedly not to investigate this whole family of concepts nor to take a stand on all, or even the major philosophical issues that have concerned it. We intend to study the concept of potentiality in particular, especially as it figures in educational thinking. In doing so, however, we shall inevitably touch on aspects of the larger family of concepts to which potentiality belongs. On such occasions, we shall strive to make our assumptions explicit and our point of view plain.

I

HUMAN NATURE AND VALUE

A. POTENTIAL IN PRACTICE AND ITS MYTHS[1]

The notion of potential is not only a hoary metaphysical idea that has come down to us from ancient Greek philosophy. It is also widely operative in the thinking of parents, educators, planners and policy-makers in the contemporary world. The educational system, it is widely said, should aim at fulfilling the potentials of children. Teachers, examiners and counselors strive to assess students' potentials. Attributing the possession of given potentials to some, they deny it of others. Whereas, however, lack of a given potential precludes its realization, possession of the same potential by no means guarantees it. Thus *attribution* of potential leads to the further question of fulfillment or *realization*: What courses of study and training, what forms of practice or life experience would help given students to realize their evident potentials? This question is obviously of central importance to students, parents, educators and planners.

Nor is this the only important question by any means. For not only may improvements be sought in the ways we try to *realize* a potential in fact possessed by a given student or group of students. We may strive also to help students *attain* potentials they have hitherto lacked. Possession as well as realization may, in other words, vary over time. A student now possessed of a given potential may or may not realize it in the future; but, also, a student now lacking such a potential may or may not come to possess it later on. The question of *enhancement* of a student's potentials

10

thus goes beyond the question of their attribution or denial at a specific time. It follows that, while the present lack of a given potential indeed precludes its realization now, it does not preclude its realization at a later time, when the potential in question may have been acquired.

This point is also, clearly, of critical importance to students, parents, teachers and planners: the stock of potentials changes over time. *The idea of fixed potentials is a myth.* It is only if the fact of change is ignored and the student's assessed potentials indeed taken as fixed and durable traits that his evident lacks may be routinely mistaken for permanent educational deficiencies. The variation over time, whether of potentials or their realizations, has two important features requiring our immediate notice: the first is the contingency of such variation on human effort; the second is the influence of a given variation on later variations.

As to the contingency of variation on human effort, we have earlier mentioned the important question, 'What courses of study and training, what forms of practice or life experience would help given students to realize their evident potentials?' The presupposition of this question is that human activities of one or another sort may make a difference to realization. The design of appropriate studies, the provision of suitable training or experience, the will to learn and practice, all these, and yet other forms of effort may, in fact, vitally affect not only the realization, but also the enhancement of potential. Thus, both what people potentially are and what they in fact turn out to be are contingent, to an incalculable extent, on human intention, both individual and social, bounded only by available resources and the limits of ingenuity. The burden of educational responsibility imposed on students, parents, teachers, planners, and indeed all society's members, stems from this fact.

The second significant feature of variation, noted above, is that a given variation typically influences subsequent ones. Potentials and their realizations are not isolated and discrete but intricately linked to one another. A girl who is potentially good at mathematics becomes a different person with actual achievement of mathematical skill. New potentials arise with the realization of the old; ways of thinking about related topics are now open to her, that were formerly closed. New feelings of confidence may contribute to potentials for other sorts of learning as well. Realiz-

11

ation, in short, is prospective and not merely retrospective. It gives rise to fresh potentials at the same time that it consummates earlier ones.

The mere enhancement of potential in one area may moreover facilitate enhancement in another. A boy who has learned enough of a foreign language to be a potential translator of elementary texts has arrived at a new plateau; it is now easier for him than before to acquire the potential to translate more advanced texts or to compare the language in question analytically with his native tongue. The cunningly ordered sequence of potentials and realizations in any educational direction that may be chosen demands of the chooser foresight, breadth of vision, and a steady sense of value. Foresight, because every educational change of state opens up new learning options it is well to anticipate; breadth of vision, because these options do not lie on a straight line determined by the initial subject, but radiate into different sectors of life; a steady sense of value, because the choice of direction requires a grasp of complex alternative goods for comparison with one another, all more or less remote from the urgencies of the present. Foresight, vision and value constitute the major part of wisdom; the task of the educator is thus revealed as rooted neither in convention, nor in craft, nor in caprice, but in a wisdom that unites knowledge, imagination and the good.

We have been discussing the *enhancement* of potential. But we must also acknowledge the *shrinkage* of available potentials. Certain educational moments must be caught or they are gone forever. William James taught that character formation is a hardening of habits, 'that by the age of thirty, the character has set like plaster, and will never soften again.'[2] The moral he drew is that the nervous system, which functions thus, is to be made an ally of education rather than its enemy – education is to instill as many useful habits as early as possible, so that the hardening of character may then proceed in a desirable direction by its own momentum.

James' formulation of the point is no doubt overstated but it strikingly expresses a general and genuine concern of educators. The capacity to learn is not an unlimited resource which can be lightly squandered. The child's curiosity, sufficiently blocked, may be dulled beyond awakening. The impulse to question, thwarted repeatedly, may eventually die. The flexibility of mind, adventuresomeness and confidence required for exploring the novel are precious and fragile learning instruments that lose their edge with disuse or abuse.

Moreover, aside from character and intellect, the existence of critical intervals for learning must be considered in widely diverse areas of education. Chess, the violin and ballet must be learned early in life, not late; aspects of the visual system mature only within the bounds of relevant critical periods; beyond another such period, any learning of a new language will, in all probability, carry with it the acquisition of a spoken accent. Potentials here today may, in short, be gone tomorrow.

The educator needs thus not only to anticipate and promote the emergence of potentials not yet in evidence; he must also try to capitalize to the fullest on potentials now manifest but shortly to disappear. He must combine a hopeful imagination of the students' future potentials with a realistic appreciation of those potentials now, but perhaps only temporarily, possessed. Striving to overcome present lacks through future possibilities, the educator is also constantly haunted by the specter of past opportunity wasted. The pressure of educational time forces him to look in both directions at once.

The mention of wasted opportunity will be instantly recognized by every reflective parent and teacher as marking a basic preoccupation. Time is so short, resources so few, education so precious in shaping the child's life: has everything possible been done to nurture the fragile growth? The child's own view is foreshortened, its sense of time and change truncated, the things populating its world taken for granted as fixed. Illusions of the rightness and durability of the given have yet to be tempered by further experience. The child cannot be expected to be sensitive to the question of wasted opportunity. But to concerned parents and teachers viewing the child against the backdrop of a longer and more realistic time line, the question can never be far below the surface.

And it is a question that is often formulated in terms of the concept of potential. Of the child's potentials, have we passed the critical period for any that are important? Have we failed to spot or appreciate crucial potentials through our own blindness? Have valuable potentials remained hidden through lack of general knowledge or lack of social interest? Have apathy, or poverty, or bias, or misguided policy thwarted the appraisal of children's

13

potentials and cruelly closed off their life prospects? Such worries, natural to parents and teachers, are central also to the concerns of society at large, for, what opens and closes the life prospects of children determines the direction and quality of society itself. Thus the process of educational planning, through which a society mediates its treatment of children's potentials, is in its style and scope an index of the society's self-image.

The press of educational responsibility is indeed heavy and relentless. Demanding relief, the educational decision-maker would welcome any way to lighten the load, to lessen the onus of choice. The tendency to replace wisdom with technology thus becomes understandable, promising to reduce the subtleties of complex decision to the simplicities of formula. We have earlier noted the simplifying myth of fixed potentials, which still thrives in various quarters, though defeated by the facts of change.[3]

Another strategy of relief from responsibility is to hide the need for discriminating among the potentials of a student – to assume them all harmoniously realizable. *This is the myth of harmonious potentials*, according to which the educator need not evaluate alternative potentials for prospective realization. His job is simply to identify the potentials that are there, and then to promote the realization of all in the most efficient manner. Maximal self-realization is the goal, understood as the fulfillment of all of one's potentials – the goal of '*being*,' as the saying goes, 'all that one *can* be.'[4]

The problem of education, thus understood, is largely emptied of its evaluative aspects and reduced to a question of fact coupled with a question of technology. The question of fact is: 'What potentials does the student have?' The question of technology is: 'How are these potentials most efficiently to be realized?' Both questions can, in principle, be turned over to scientific investigation for resolution and the educator's task reduced to doing whatever the investigation concludes will most efficiently realize all the student's potentials, there being some such self-realizing course available in every case. Thus are the main functions of education reduced to *finding* the potentials and then *realizing* them forthwith.

Comforting as this picture has been both for educational theorists and practitioners, it is fatally flawed. William James expressed the main point when he somewhere remarked that the philosopher

14

and the lady-killer cannot both keep house in the same tenement of clay.[5] The potential for the one career and the potential for the other may both be genuinely *possessed* by a given youth but that does not imply that he has the potential for both together. Thus, they are not, alas, jointly *realizable*. Merely to *identify* these potentials is thus not sufficient to warrant the attempt at realization. For to realize the one has the effect of precluding the other, the two being unrealizable together. If one is to be preferred to the other, there must be a judgment embodying such preference. And such judgment will reflect the relative values ascribed to conflicting realizations.

Every student in fact harbors potentials that are as such compatible but whose realizations conflict. One cannot literally be all that one can be; there are fundamentally different lives that anyone might live, depending on the choices made by oneself and others – and it is true of many such lives that each excludes the rest. Choice precludes as well as includes; there is no blinking this fact and, consequently, no relief from educational responsibility in the notion of a comprehensive fulfillment of all one's potentials.

Nor does this notion represent the only way in which the concept of potential is employed so as to lessen the pressure of choice. We have been discussing the proper attribution and enhancement of potential, the reduction or shrinkage of potential, the discovery and development of hidden potentials, and the efficient realization of potentials. In every one of these cases, the potentials in question are assumed to have positive value and their realizations to represent goods as well. *This is the myth of uniformly valuable potentials* which, once questioned, is seen to be groundless. People are potentially evil as well as good. They are potentially considerate but also potentially callous, potentially kind and potentially cruel, potentially sensitive and potentially boorish, potentially insightful and intelligent, and potentially obtuse and stupid. We need, in short, to take account not only of incompatible values but also of positive disvalues.

In the typical practical employment of the language of potential, these negative aspects are all filtered out. It is not noted that the educator's aim is to destroy as well as to strengthen potentials, to shrink as well as to enhance various sorts, to block as well as to promote their realization. Propped by the classical philosophical tradition in which the concept of potential was originally nurtured, this reading of the concept accentuates the positive, fostering the illusion that no value discriminations by the educator are needed. All that wants doing is the factual identification of existent potentials, all to be promoted since all worthy – all aspects of the real, or higher self to be realized in education.[6]

Further consideration of this philosophical background will be attempted in the chapter to follow. At this point, enough has been said about the notion of potential in educational practice to pinpoint its main functions therein, and to allow us to raise a general question: what features of human nature underlie these functions, making the practical uses of the notion of potential understandable?

B. HUMAN NATURE AND POTENTIAL

An answer to the above question will help us to appreciate the functions of education itself, as well as the practical role of the concept of potential. Such appreciation will, in turn, provide a basis for reconstruction of the concept in light of philosophical criticisms to be considered in the next chapter. For these criticisms, damaging as they may be to the traditional concept of potential, do not alleviate the needs which this concept has met in practice, however inadequately. A sympathetic grasp of such needs as flowing from distinctive features of human nature will help to keep our eventual reconstruction sensitive to practice as it strives for dialectical adequacy.

We proceed then to sketch a general account of human nature that we take to be empirically sound and that we shall presuppose in our later discussions as providing a proper context for educational policy. This account characterizes human action as mediated by intention, belief and symbolism. It offers a teleological interpretation of action, in terms of belief, on the one hand, and goals, purposes or desires, on the other. It elaborates the temporal character of action, the way it binds particular pasts to particular futures. Discussing the role of norms in self and society, it outlines the creation of new norms through decision and reinterpretation. Finally, the account stresses the role of value and emotion in all action.[7]

1. *Change, Action and Symbolic Representation*

Ordinary references to human potential acknowledge change in human lives. What is potential at one time may be realized at another. A person's potentials are the seeds of possible changes in his powers and attainments. A familiar connotation of 'potential,' moreover, is that of changes mediated by intentions and beliefs, whether of oneself or of others.

The concept of change mediated by intention and belief introduces the notion of *action*, performed with a certain outcome in view but carrying further consequences in its train. Among these consequences may be those for the sake of which the action was initiated. However, these actual consequences may fail to include any of those initially envisaged, the action carried through under a false anticipation. And even where expected consequences do in fact occur, they are typically accompanied by others, not foreseen and calling for improved anticipations in the future. The interplay between envisaged outcomes and actual effects is a basic fact of human action.[8]

Human action in fact presupposes capacities that far outreach those of other animals. Foremost among such capacities is that of *symbolic representation*, in virtue of which intentions may be expressed, anticipations formulated, purposes projected and past outcomes recalled. Human beings are, in consequence, not constrained in their development as are their fellow creatures. Their lives are not bounded by the reach of their instincts and drives, coupled with the opportunities and challenges of their physical environments; they do not live in the immediate present alone, responding only to contemporary forces playing upon them. Human beings are symbolic animals, hence both creators and creatures of culture, capable of memory, imagination, fear and hope, interpreters of the world and of themselves, choosers among options they themselves define, and vulnerable as well to the choices of their fellows. Such interpretations and choices make a fateful difference to the direction and quality of a human life. What the biology of the infant leaves open at birth is, in short, filled out by culture, history, education and decision.

That human action is neither physical movement nor biological development or response alone, but is rather symbolic in character, is a basic fact from which far-reaching consequences

17

flow. For the symbolic systems constructed by human beings are not simply changes rung upon some universal matrix, itself sprung from the givens of physics. These several systems are each underdetermined by physical fact, and there is no principle that guarantees perfect harmony and coordination among them. That a given person acts under the aegis of a particular symbolic system is therefore a fact about that person of the first significance, deducible neither from his natural environment nor from his biological equipment, and implying what cannot be simply inferred from other symbolic systems. It means that his action can be understood only if we make an effort to understand the system of categories *he* takes to be applicable to his situation, the features *he* selects for notice, the alternatives he faces, as *he* would describe them.

By *symbolic systems*, we have in mind clusters of categories or terms which a person typically deploys in certain contexts. Aside from *terms*, we include also non-linguistic vehicles of representation, comprehending the graphical or diagrammatic, the pictorial and plastic, the kinetic and the ritual. What symbolic systems share is the function of ostensible reference to features selected for notice, and of consequent sensitization to properties and relations, inclusions, exclusions, hierarchies and contrasts which organize the world of the subject in characteristic ways. To comprehend an action requires that we not only place it in its environment as analyzed by *our* categories, but realize how the *subject* sees things, how *the subject* organizes the field within which the action takes place.[9]

2. Action, Belief and Purpose

Beyond the symbolic system, i.e. the referential equipment of the subject, we need further to consider how he uses it to characterize his situation. It is, clearly, not only his vocabulary that is important; it is of critical importance how he *applies* this vocabulary in articulating his beliefs and formulating his purposes. Action is indeed always mediated by belief and qualified by want or purpose. Without knowing what the subject hopes to accomplish and how he supposes that what he does will help to realize such hope, his action must, in a clear sense, remain opaque to us. Conversely, to comprehend his action typically involves locating it within the field composed of the subject's beliefs and goals, seeing the action, no matter how deflected by independent factors, as at least a putative means (according to these beliefs) to the ends in question.

Such interpretation of the action is teleological; it tells us not whether the action was in fact *successful*, but rather what the subject was *trying* to accomplish and what his rationale was. Teleological explanations have, it is true, been largely expunged from the natural sciences, since it is no longer acceptable to attribute beliefs or purposes to physical objects. Such explanations are, however, of enduring relevance in the human sciences, history, literature and everyday life, where the beliefs and purposes of people are of major interest in characterizing and predicting their conduct. It is not that reference to beliefs and goals of the agent *wholly* accounts for the action in question, which may in fact deviate from his intent, for various reasons. It is rather that such intent, coupled with knowledge of deflecting factors (e.g. irrationality, inefficiency, bias, ignorance, incapacity, etc.), provides a major explanatory model for human action.[10]

The upshot is that it is not enough for us to be clear about *our own* beliefs as to the subject's environment; we must also be clear about *his* beliefs as to his environment. We must not only understand *our own* purposes, but also grasp *his* purposes. Whether we share the subject's beliefs and goals is beside the point; true or false, misguided or not from our point of view, they are elements of the factual situation that must enter into *our own* account if it is to help us comprehend *his* action.

To understand a subject's beliefs and purposes, we must, in sum, try to comprehend his symbolic system and, further, attend to his particular formulations and representations within that system, coordinating what we learn thus with what we can tell from his overt conduct. Since beliefs and purposes expressible in a natural language can exhibit endless subtlety, complexity and nuance, there is no royal road to understanding other people. One must take seriously the particularity of their beliefs and values as they themselves are inclined to express them, fitting their actions to such beliefs and values as smoothly as possible and treating the resulting interpretation as an empirical hypothesis corrigible by further experience.[11]

3. Representation of the Environment

We have stressed the agent's symbolic representation of his environment and the formulation of his own wants or purposes in the determination of his action. We are, however, not in the first instance aware of such functions in our own case; naively, the child attends to the *chair* in using the *word 'chair,'* not pausing to ponder the word. Our native tongue appears to us at the beginning as a purely transparent window on the real world.[12] Only later on, in encountering other tongues and other usages do we come to a more reflective self-consciousness about our own symbolic representations. Extended further, such self-consciousness turns systematically critical, forcing a theoretical wedge between ourselves and our own representations, imposing on such representations whatever far-reaching and indirect tests can be invented by the skeptical scientific spirit. Although we can never extricate ourselves from our own symbolism, never see things completely bare of representation, we do thus acquire a reflective distance from our representative functions. Through learning and comparing other symbolic systems than those we were born into, and through acquiring scientifically critical attitudes, we can come to understand that people in general, and we too among them, live in a symbolic environment, constituted not alone of physical things but of beliefs and purposes that may themselves do more than simply reflect such things.

Thus the notion we have heretofore employed – that symbolisms *represent* the environment – is too simple; it suggests that variant schemes differ simply in differently classifying real things independently known to us. But some beliefs are false, some postulate things that never were on land or sea, some imagine things that could not exist in any possible world. These beliefs represent no actual environment; yet they are no less effective for all that in the determination of action. A person with such beliefs is living in a special symbolic medium. This medium does not just *represent* the agent's environment; it is *part of* it. The symbolic component of a person's environment does not simply reflect the rest; it is itself creative, spilling over the bounds of other actualities to add its own particular portion.

Even waiving the question of false and incoherent beliefs, the idea of symbolism representing *the* environment requires considerable complication. It is not as if there is some fixed array of objects in the subject's local environment, which are organized or described in one or another way, depending on his symbolic system and his beliefs. The concept of 'the environment' is an enormously elastic one, contracting or expanding without definite assignable limits under variant circumstances. While non-human animals at best 'map' only a relatively small spatio-temporal surround, the advent of symbolism makes possible reference to an indefinitely large region of space and time. Beliefs about the remote past as well as the outer reaches of the universe, assumptions about the history of one's forebears and suppositions as to the long-range future of one's people, of humanity or, indeed, of the universe as a whole, enter into the thinking of human beings in a way that is unimaginable for creatures without language.

Language is, moreover, a social product and a social phenomenon through and through. We must not fall into the easy misconception that only physical space-time or physical attributes are available for reference. On the contrary, of major importance in the environment of each of us are the beliefs and purposes of other people, to which our language makes it possible to refer. These beliefs and purposes may belong to persons as close to us as members of our own families or as distant as the ancient Athenians or the contemporary or future members of a remote civilization. The powerful influence of written traditions carrying the heritage of the past across the generations is testimony to the way human environments far outstrip the local physical surround of their subjects. But writing is only an intensification of the capacity of all speech and, indeed, of symbolism in general to crystallize references to things far outside the local scene of action. Since the beliefs made possible by symbolism in turn become objects of the beliefs of others, we become infinitely reflecting mirrors to one another in society.

It is the reference to things far removed from the local scene that gives body to our earlier comment that human beings do not live in the immediate present alone, responding only to the contemporary forces playing upon them. For saints and martyrs, revolutionaries and tyrants, thinkers and poets, statesmen and generals, artists and teachers, peasants and priests, the operative environments represented in their beliefs comprise worlds that can by no stretch of the imagination be contained within the local scene of their actions. Now it is true that the beliefs and purposes relevant to a given action are *themselves* contemporaneous with it, even though the *objects to which they refer* may antecede or follow it. Nevertheless, since there is no way to characterize a belief or purpose except through reference to its putative objects, we must ourselves, of necessity, enter into the extended temporal world of the agent in order to account for his or her action. We must understand the operative religious past of saint and martyr, the events that live on in revolutionary ideologies, the futures conceived by statesmen and poets, the works of the past that still inspire thinkers, artists and peasants.

4. Action and Time-binding

It should not be thought mysterious that the scene of human action thus runs both backward and forward from the immediate present. For all action links past and future, organizing or 'binding' time in a characteristic way.[13] Performed with a certain outcome in view and with further consequences anticipated, an action starts out with implicit reference to the future. But it also involves an estimate of prevailing conditions in virtue of which the action to be performed is deemed to have a good chance of succeeding. And such judgment itself, whether sound or not, purports to find its basis in past trials or past testimony. After the action has been performed, moreover, the predicted outcome and associated consequences provide a basis for retrospective appraisal. Occurring as predicted at the predicted times, they confirm the original anticipations; failing to occur, they disconfirm them. In either case they allow evaluation of the past action, which may tend either to strengthen or to weaken its underlying impulses in the future.

All action thus involves memory and imagination, both at the point of initiation and at the time of later reflection. It finds its significance through taking some present course as pathway to an imagined future, in light of some recollected past. The impact of a developed symbolism is immeasurably to extend the rudimentary native capacity of memory and imagination to enter into, and thus to qualify human action.

Purposes may accordingly take infinitely many forms, imagination shaping action through the infinitely expressive language available to the agent. To become a computer scientist, or an oboist, or a Guinness record holder for keeping a pipe going the longest, are purposes hardly conceivable without language. They connect, respectively, with different courses of action selected by different ranges of recollection. Such recollection advises what one must do if one really wants to become a computer scientist, or an oboist, or a Guinness pipe smoking record holder. Such advice, too, is unimaginable without language.

In the foregoing examples, purposes initially fixed guided the selection of appropriate pasts. It is also true, conversely, that pasts initially internalized guide the adoption of suitable purposes. Moreover, actions entered upon with only a dim sense of their significance may tend in due course to seek out both relevant pasts and futures, binding them ever more tightly together.

The purposes we have here taken as illustrations are individual in nature; they exemplify career choices or attempts to set individual records in competition. Even such choices, however, take place in a social context with a past. The career possibilities that beckon have been formed earlier and the records to be broken are records already set. Present choice connects the agent to a special social past and directs him toward a particular social future. It sharpens his definition as an agent that he has chosen thus; his individuality emerges more clearly in the binding of time effected by his act.

The aspiring oboist thus differs from the aspiring computer scientist or farmer or ballet dancer. But the choice to become an oboist does not wholly mark him off from others. He shares the past references and the future visions of other intending oboists, who by similar choices have selected the same precedents to follow, the same standards to uphold and perhaps surpass. Of course, each oboist is not just an oboist but a fully rounded person – choosing continuously in every dimension of life, and by the whole organization of such choices achieving an individualized identity. But such identity is perfectly compatible with social commonalities, with the shared binding of time that relates individuals to one another.

Such sharing is most clearly shown by communities, nations, societies, cultures. As distinct from abstract career groupings, such units encompass people in living interaction with one another,

23

who share a common experience and a common fate. The actions taken by a community or nation are those taken by its institutional authorities. Such actions are also oriented toward future outcomes, and relate to estimates of present circumstances and memories of past efforts. But they do not affect just the individual leaders involved. Unlike the career choices of the previous example, these actions carry everyone in the group along, independently of their several intentions. Such actions often have longer time perspectives, covering decades or generations rather than months or years. The interests of a society as interpreted by its authorities may, further, invite actions requiring concerted efforts across several lifetimes. Such considerations show a stronger and broader time-binding than we have hitherto discussed. Common memories coordinated with common aspirations linked by common efforts in succeeding generations – such are the bonds that mold and hold communities.

This social fabric of time recalled and time envisaged forms the background against which smaller-scale individual choices are made. It provides a common framework of reference for the lives lived within its scope, and comes to have, for these lives, such an obviousness as to make it virtually unquestioned, almost wholly unnoticed. Yet different societies live by different memories. They select different pasts and take these pasts to counsel different actions, in the service of different aspirations. Without special efforts to understand, the contacts between different societies may resemble the conversations of the deaf. In sum, communities bind; they also divide. The same symbolic structure that binds a society together across time serves also to separate it from societies otherwise bound, via other symbolisms.

5. *Rules, Self, Norms and Criticism*

We have been emphasizing the selective temporal references that enter into action. But this is hardly the whole role of symbolism in human life. The great eighteenth-century philosopher, Immanuel Kant, taught that whereas 'everything in nature works in accordance with laws, only a rational being has the capacity of acting in accordance with his conception of laws, i.e. according to principles.'[14] Human beings formulate rules or laws for themselves by which they monitor their own conduct, and create ideals to which they try to conform. Such functions go beyond the mere having of beliefs and purposes; here the effect is reflexive: the agent strives to meet a standard, to conform to a style, to approximate an ideal. What emerges here is implicit self-reference, awareness of how one is acting, whether one has in fact performed properly, whether one has lived up to one's ideal. Such self-reference implies that the agent has, as G. H. Mead put it, 'become an object to himself,' has swept himself into the sphere of his own reference.[15] He has attained a form of self-consciousness, and with it the ability to attend to, and to correct, his conduct in light of his rules and ideals. This remarkable ability, born of symbolic capacity, is the root of self-criticism, the precondition both of science and of conscience.

The development of self-knowledge, as Mead emphasized, grows out of the social process. The child, initially unself-conscious, comes to be aware of itself through the reactions of others to its acts. We first learn about ourselves through seeing our reflections in the eyes and attitudes of others; concurrently, we learn to act so as to evoke the favorable responses of others. The growth of self-awareness and the internalizing of social norms thus go hand in hand. Once begun, such processes have no natural limit. Awareness of oneself as an agent *relative to* one's social norms may turn into awareness of oneself as *responsible for* one's social norms. These norms in this way lose their status as ultimate sanctions of choice and themselves become objects of a choice to be made reflectively on independent grounds. The sense of agency no longer merely operates by social norms but reacts upon them and transcends them in its further legislation of principles. Self-awareness has, in sum, become fully critical.

6. Education, Self-awareness and Value

Self-awareness is a recognized aim of education, which has as one of its main purposes the preservation and improvement of the structure of social rules and ideals. This is not to say, however, that conflicts do not occur over the realization of this aim. Self-awareness is strong medicine; once it cures the patient of dogmatic ignorance of his own powers, it releases energies that may be turned against the social structure itself. Once appeal is made to the student's understanding of principles, he may see the improvement of the social structure differently from the way it is typically seen. Socrates, the great saint and martyr of education, was condemned to death by his fellow Athenians for corrupting the youth. What they saw as corruption was corrosion of the old ways and beliefs. What Socrates taught, on the other hand, was the pursuit of wisdom, of critical self-knowledge which constitutes not only man's highest religious duty but a sure improvement in the ways of the state.[16]

We come now face to face with the matter of value and its relation to action as we have characterized it. For the conflict in ancient Athens over the meaning of Socrates' career was a conflict over the good, and wherever action becomes reflective, it touches upon questions of good. Action was earlier characterized as involving belief and desire; the choice initiating an action is made with a wanted outcome in view, for the sake of consequences brought in its train. Socrates thought that no one could knowingly choose the worse of two alternatives, for in the very act of deliberate choice, he implies that the alternative acted upon is, in his judgment, better than the one rejected. Thus if someone does in fact choose the worse over the better course, the reason must lie in ignorance. Aristotle differed on this point, holding that even full knowledge does not guarantee that choice will fasten upon the good; choice is a matter not of knowledge alone but also of the will, and weakness of will may deflect choice from its proper object, even if such object is accurately evaluated.[17] For Socrates, then, all action is directed toward what is deemed good while, for Aristotle, this is not so, but even Aristotle's weak-willed man is one who knows that he has fallen short of the good. In so far as his choice is deliberate, it too involves a judgment as to the good. But what the good itself involves is a matter of deep philosophical controversy.

What is less controversial is that, however interpreted, a value assertion or ethical claim is one that goes beyond mere desire. To say that a book or movie is good is to say more than just that one likes it; if I say an act is right, I claim more than that it is congenial to me. There is here a connotation of intersubjectivity, an implicit invitation to the hearer to see for himself whether in fact the claim is not correct as advanced. Philosophical theories differ in how

26

they interpret the content of such claims but not, for the most part, in seeing this content as involving more than just desire.[18] Now it seems plausible to say that the language of value is learned, in the first instance, as an overlay on the language of wants. Action initially directed merely to the satisfaction of wants is modified by socialization which sets limits both on means and on ends. Action socialized is action performed not only to satisfy individual desire but action fitting the general expectations of the community. It has now become minimally reflective, for it is action set in a social context demanding consideration. Where community expectations are themselves vague or incompatible, or in competition with rival community allegiances, reflection goes further and deeper; the pursuit of an intersubjective good reaches beyond particular communities toward the universal.

In both these phases, desire remains a critical element of action. It is not that socialization merely curbs desire by external force, although it may do that at the outset. Rather, it transforms desire, so that the child wants what its parents want for it to want. The birth of consideration and social tact is here, when the child begins to want social approval in a way that modifies others of its wants, and has to reflect on what such approval entails. And when deliberation on action goes beyond socialization toward a universal notion of the good, it again transforms desire rather than eliminating or curbing it as a component of action. It demands of the agent the modification of other desires by the desire to meet some universal standard.

A value statement or ethical claim, we have said, goes beyond mere desire. Yet now we say that desire continues to remain an essential element of action. Is there a contradiction here? Not if we are careful to distinguish value *claims* from *explanations* of associated actions. To make a value claim is to indicate more than merely that the speaker has a certain desire; it is to say further that the object of the claim meets some additional, independent condition, for example, that it is socially approved or passes some universalistic test, however conceived. A value claim is in itself, however, neither a description nor an explanation of an action.

If we now assert the speaker to have acted in such a way as to bring this object into being, or to promote or support its existence, we are interpreting his action as directed toward a certain purpose; we are saying, to put it roughly, that he wants to promote value, or (if we dissociate ourselves from his claim) that he wants to promote what he considers value. In either case, we have reference to his desire in understanding his act. His motivation, in other words, remains an essential aspect of our teleological account of his action; it is just that its object is one that is asserted to incorporate the special marks of value. There is thus no contradiction between value and desire. It is in fact a cardinal aim of education so to transform initial desire as to favor its fastening upon value.

7. Norm-internalization and Norm-creation

The child, we have said, internalizes social norms. But norms are in general not transmitted without change, and new norms are always in process of creation. Nor is such creation always a matter of explicit statement. If the internalization metaphor is inadequate, the model of legislation is not a sufficient alternative. John Dewey has, in a related connection, stressed the generation of forms or standards out of experience itself, both in the sciences and the arts.[19] And R. M. Hare has shown how particular decisions occasioned by new experience embody generalizations; hence his telling phrase, 'decisions of principle.'[20] No decision is ever wholly isolated, or restricted to its own situation. Every decision echoes or reverberates outward. The considerations going into it, once made explicit, or even half-explicit, have implications for other situations and create the felt need for consistency and integrity of judgment.

We need not therefore suppose norms to spring full-blown into existence. Starting with the background of social norms into which each of us is born, we are forced into choices by the contingencies of life, choices never wholly covered by such norms. These choices, in so far as they are reflective, require analysis of the relevant circumstances, partition of alternatives, analogies to the past and to similar cases, identification of relevant features attending possible courses of action. Once made, a choice fixes certain of these aspects, favors certain precedents, strengthens particular analogies, etc. and, moreover, creates new precedents for future action. Here the generalization of choice is evident.

28

Such generalization is the basis of – indeed constitutes – a norm, a rule or principle.

Choices are inevitably systematic in import; they create new norms and contribute to the amending of old. Even where guided by prior norms, they typically help to alter such norms by revising the set of precedents and operative analogies available. The development of codes of law out of case law and the continuous reinterpretation of codes in response to new cases illustrate well the processes we have been describing. Nor are these processes restricted either to the law or to fundamental social norms. From a very early age onward, a child learns to recognize the generalizing force of precedents embodied in specific decisions. Told by his parents on Tuesday that he may stay up on that day an hour later than his usual bedtime, he will want to know why he cannot continue this practice on Wednesday. Unless the parents produce some convincing distinction compatible with accumulated precedents in the child's experience, they will stand charged with inconsistency. And any distinction newly introduced will change the body of rules operative henceforth.

As each action tends to generalize itself into a rule, it purports to comprehend similar cases in the past and also to guide choice in similar cases in the future: being committed to a rule, moreover, promotes the sense of consistency over time of a durable agent, whether individual self or structured community. This sense of enduring consistency requires continual monitoring if it is to be maintained. The challenge of new contingencies of decision requires a re-reading of old precedent. Even where a society simply rejects the challenge, it will need to take steps to reinforce the lesson of old precedent. Once it decides to take the new challenge seriously, it is embarked on a process of reinterpreting its past so as to find new bonds of continuity between its tradition and the emerging problems of life. Perhaps the most central and poignant challenges facing contemporary societies can be understood in these terms.

Symbolic capacity makes symbolic systems possible. It also makes possible the process of reinterpretation which accounts for the characteristics of such a system at any given moment in history. In emphasizing that human beings are creators of culture, we mean neither that each person produces a culture, nor that whatever effect a person does have is by promulgating a set of norms outright. Rather, by the innumerable and continuing collection of individual choices made by human beings, the norms which circumscribe their lives are developed and reworked. Of course not every choice is as weighty as every other, the institutions of society assigning power differentially to different choices. But the fact remains that the culture in force at any time is a product of human choice, constrained by circumstance, while correspondingly conditioning further choice within its ambit. If human beings create culture in this sense, they are also its creatures, for the symbolic systems qualifying their choices are cultural products.

Choices presuppose possibilities, that is to say, options. Now the set of considered options is a product of culture, in particular, of the symbolic reinterpretive process leading up to the moment of choice. In providing this set, culture defines the possibilities of action for each agent. But it must not be supposed that there is a sharp opposition here between culture and the individual agent. For culture comprises the whole reinterpretive process leading up to the choice in question, and this includes also all previous choices that may have been made by the agent himself. He too is part of the culture which shapes the conditions of his action.

The division is not between culture and the individual, but between the accumulated effects of prior choices on present options and the choice now made – between options already created, by the agent or others, and the option now selected. The option selected contributes to the creation of the considered array subsequently available; thus option selection and option creation are not sealed off from one another but interact in a continuous process. Since each option selected by an agent affects the possibilities of his future action, he helps thus to define the very game in which he will later play, or, better, to redefine with each of his moves the very game in which he has been a player from birth.

8. *Action and Emotion: Foresight, Fear and Hope*

We have characterized action in terms of norms and choices. But we must not lose sight of the pervasive role of emotions in all action. Kant, to whom we have referred, held that in morally principled action, one curbs one's natural fears and self-love in deference to the rule of morality to which one has bound oneself.

Respect for the moral law is, for Kant, an emotion, by which other emotions are to be governed.[21] Respect for one's principles and ideals indeed has concomant emotional consequences: living up to such principles and ideals is a source of well-being while violations and lapses occasion remorse or shame.[22]

Action on principle requires a certain courage, the ability to withstand natural fears of unpleasant consequences following upon such action. A child who is learning to tell the truth is learning to overcome the fear of such consequences. But in acquiring the principle of truth-telling, the child is learning respect for the moral law, which itself involves a certain sort of fear. Such respect, as Kant analyzes it, involves both *love*, that is, recognition that the law is not imposed from without but has an independent source within one's rational self, and *fear*, that is, acknowledgment that the law binds one, and requires to be obeyed no matter what one's momentary inclinations may be.[23] Fear is thus, in the course of moral education, detached from its initial natural objects and attached to moral principles. Analogously, love comes to be attached to such principles, with their dawning recognition in the child's consciousness.

Now action, as we have considered it, is oriented by desire toward a certain outcome and selected consequences envisaged to flow from it. As John Dewey has rightly emphasized, there is a continuum of ends and means involved in deliberations over action.[24] The consequences of an act are not separated from one another nor are they sharply divided from the action itself which initiates their production. Further, they are not cleanly bounded by some perimeter lying on the horizon of the future. Rather, they fade outward in every direction, losing definiteness and certainty with distance. Dewey used the notion of the continuum as an aid in criticism of desire, a way of helping transform mere desire into the desirable. Consider the further consequences of what you desire, he counsels, consider the cost of the means, take account of the side-effects of your action and their costs, consider what sort of person you will become in carrying through the action you contemplate.

Nevertheless, the importance of desire remains; the critique is not meant to expunge it but only to refine it and broaden its base. The instrument of such critique, for Dewey, is empirical knowledge, yielding foresight as to the consequences of action.

31

Such knowledge of the consequences of what we do is, for Dewey, the central goal of scientific inquiry; such knowledge is at the same time the main source of insight into the meaning of our actions and the basis for understanding the environment which responds to them. Scientific knowledge is of *relations*, between act and consequence, between one consequence and a further one, between actions and side-effects; and grasp of such relations yields, at the moment of choice initiating action, *foresight* as to the continuous flow of diverse effects that may be expected of it, such foresight constituting an understanding of the *meaning* of the action. Foresight as to such meaning enters into the present choice, modifies it through enlightenment, and enables its refinement through increased control.[25]

But Dewey's account presupposes desire throughout, as providing preferences capable of ranking and selecting among consequences anticipated by foresight. Without such preferences, foresight alone would not empower choice. With such preferences, foresight in fact broadens, illuminates and strengthens its capability. The problem of value, for Dewey, is not to derive preference from 'pure' fact, but to find a way of refining and harmonizing preferences that may be presumed to exist in the living organism from the very beginning.[26] The conception of science that Dewey espouses is one that emphasizes its usefulness in such refinement and harmonization. In providing the requisite foresight, science, broadly conceived, helps us grasp the meaning of our actions. It is, in this sense, humanistic in its function and focus though of course objective in its aims and methods, for it could not fulfill its function without providing correctives to our short-sightedness, ignorance and wishful thinking.

Now the desire uniformly involved in action is itself an emotion and it is linked to other emotions. Kant's discussion concerns moral principles, but it is important to remember that morality does not exhaust questions of choice; it provides an overarching framework within which an infinite number of diverse choices are possible, compatible with its requirements. The particular actions we take, the projects we plan – if not immoral – engage our emotions in ways that go beyond, although compatible with, our moral emotions.

A young man or woman enters upon a career, decides to become a physician or a teacher or engineer. Morality in itself has nothing to say about the choice. Each career is compatible with the moral law in the abstract. Yet the decision, a corollary of initial desire on the part of the agent, that is, of the initial attractiveness to the agent of the career chosen, enlists further emotion in its aftermath. Based on present estimates of what the decision will bring about, the initial decision cannot guarantee the truthfulness of such estimates. The decision must be taken in the face of uncertainty and it must therefore be supported by hope, the hope that desired consequences will ensue, a hope that will be realistic in proportion as it merges with scientific expectation based on experience.

Correspondingly, there will be apprehension or fear of disappointment, realistic to the extent warranted by empirically founded foresight. Both hope and fear may be realistic or exaggerated – even irrational. But that some element of both is involved in every choice, every action or project, is difficult to deny.

As the studies required for the student's chosen career progress, the sense of its content and significance alters, the demands enlarge and become more specific, the costs in effort become plain. To bear these costs means that the object of desire is capable of overriding them even with an enlarged perception of what is involved. Desire here blossoms into commitment, perseverance, loyalty – a kind of love of the project embarked on, with which one identifies oneself and which helps shape one's self-respect. Beyond realistic hope, not always available, lies faith; and love of the goal may inspire the courage to conquer even realistic fears. It is not only in the realm of moral principle, thus, that fear and love, courage and respect, have a role to play, but throughout the sphere of action their relevance is evident. Hedged about by constraints on available options, by limitations of capability, and by the uncertainty of even the best-available foresight, human choice proceeds nevertheless to stake out paths in the jungle of possibilities, building habitations of varied structure and adornment to house its loves and works.

33

C. NORMATIVE ASSUMPTIONS: VALUES STUDIED AND VALUES PRESUPPOSED

The account of human nature we have presented centers on action, which in turn has been interpreted as involving desire, intention, purpose. Whenever action becomes reflective, as we have earlier said, it touches upon questions of good – questions concerning intersubjective desirability, rather than mere desire. Now the study of human nature is itself a form of action carried out by human beings in pursuit of certain purposes. As such study itself attains self-consciousness, it must be concerned to make explicit its own underlying conceptions of the good, its claims to value and the rationale for such claims. If the account we have given of action is correct, we cannot, as students of action, pretend to a position of value-neutrality; we are caught by our own human nature in the web of value considerations and there is no remedy but to work our way through it, making each step taken as plain as possible.

We have described our work as contributing toward a practical rather than a disciplinary theory of education. For disciplinary theory, there is a reasonably familiar framework of motivating value assumptions spelled out in the literature of scientific method and philosophy of science. But this framework will not encompass the normative presuppositions needed for our task. Aside from the values of scientific understanding exemplified in scientific inquiry, we presuppose also a normative conception of the values governing educational practice, from the most individualized concerns of the teacher or tutor to the general concerns of policy-makers. In dealing with the concept of potential in particular, it is important to be especially critical with respect to value questions for, as we have earlier noted, there is a traditional tendency to read only positive values into a person's potentials, and to assume them all harmoniously realizable, thus begging the question of potentials with disvalue, and that of conflicts among potentials demanding choice.

What is meant in saying we presuppose a normative conception? In the first place, we do not mean that such a conception is implied by the empirical materials investigated and reported by our project. Nor, secondly, do we mean that our normative presuppositions themselves imply such empirical data. These presuppositions, however, qualify the way our conceptual framework is constructed and our empirical materials organized. They select special aspects for consideration, highlight certain forms of human interaction, and bring particular features of the phenomena into the foreground of attention. Knowing the normative principles behind such selectivity, the reader will be able to discern the threads integrating our presentation of the pertinent empirical materials.

But the matter goes deeper than this. The normative conception we *presuppose* in organizing the materials of disciplinary inquiry is, at the same time, an *integral part* of the practical theory we are developing. For a practical theory includes value considerations at its foundations, these considerations setting the goals of the practice in question; in our case the practical theory must state or imply a view of the goals of educational decision. Moreover, a developed theory will not only express such a view but will also offer a rationale for it, spelling out the motivating reasons behind its acceptance. This we propose to do here, thus providing the reader not only with a sense of the integrative principles behind our empirical presentations, but also with a sense of the value approach here taken and its underlying rationale.

I mentioned earlier that value assertions or ethical claims go beyond mere desire, and connote some form of intersubjectivity. To this point, I have spoken in very general terms of value, failing to distinguish moral from non-moral value, the right from the good, ethics from desirability.[27] The more specific consideration of such distinctions in the requisite detail would take us far afield, and involve us in the intricacies of the historical literature of moral philosophy. The alternative, which I choose here, is to sketch my conception, introducing only as much specificity as is required to expound it, and hoping that the omission of further detail will not be mistaken for dogmatism.

I take as starting point the earlier references to Kant, who took man's distinctive feature to be the ability to legislate rules for himself, i.e., his autonomy.[28] Nowadays, the term 'autonomy' is often vulgarly used to mean permissiveness, or *laissez-faire*, or selfishness, or egotism or lack of community feeling. None of these connotations has any place in Kant's view. 'Autonomy,' for him, is the capacity to bind oneself freely by rule or principle, to act, not just as an object, in accordance with law, but as a person, in accordance with one's conception of law.

Kant thought that all action is directed toward ends but governed by subjective rules (termed 'maxims'), that persons set for themselves. Kant's problem was to find what he called 'the supreme principle of morality,' which would serve as a test applied to maxims, serving to single out and separate immoral maxims from the rest. This principle, in Kant's treatment, turned out to be a universalization criterion: if the maxim in question cannot consistently with the relevant action be supposed to govern the action of all in similar situations, it is immoral, otherwise not.

The person in difficult straits who borrows money promising to repay, but with the intent not to repay, is acting on a maxim which if universalized would be inconsistent with the very action in question. For if everyone acted on the implicit maxim, 'When in difficult straits, borrow and promise to repay, but with the intent not to repay,' promises would not be believed, and this promise in particular could not possibly achieve its intended goal. The liar, in general, depends on the fact that, by and large, people do not lie but tell the truth, thus reinforcing the credibility that his lying communication requires in order to succeed. If people were generally to lie, our communications would not be believed, and the particular lying act would fail of its goal, i.e., to convince the hearer of the truth of the lie in question. Lying fails the universalization test and thus is immoral. However, to refrain from lying passes the test; indeed to refrain from lying is a moral imperative, a categorical imperative, in Kant's terminology, since its only alternative is to lie.

Why did Kant take universalization as a moral test? Consider the example, just given, of the liar, who hopes to accomplish his end through capitalizing on the accrued trust built up by truth-tellers. Let others be bound to tell the truth, he says, while I remain free to achieve my ends by lying. I am an exception to the general rule, and I *depend on being* an exception in achieving my end. Other people – both truth-tellers in general, and the person lied to – are treated as instruments to the achievement of the liar's end; he denies to them the privileges he takes for himself. They are thus for the liar objects, not persons. He denies them the respect due persons, which is the acknowledgment that they too, like the liar, are capable of understanding the general application of rules and, indeed, of legislating rules for governing their actions, that they therefore deserve fully equal treatment, and that the liar himself qualifies for no special or privileged treatment just because he is he.

Kant supposed the root of immorality to consist in excluding oneself from the general rules one lays down for others, in making exceptions for oneself, thus in treating people as objects or means to one's own ends rather than as ends in their own right. The Principle of the Categorical Imperative Kant thus formulated in one of its versions as follows: Act so that you treat humanity, whether in your own person or in that of another, always as an end and never as a means only.[29] This principle, embodying the Kantian notion of respect for persons, is intimately tied to the universalization test, as we have shown above. It has for Kant for further connotation that in respecting persons, hence treating them not as mere objects or means to our own ends, we treat them as choosing their own ends and acting in accordance with their own maxims just as we act on ours.

An important point to note is the way the test is supposed to operate. It declares maxims failing the test to be immoral, as is the maxim of the lying promise of Kant's example. To refrain from lying promises passes the test and is shown to be not only not immoral but, further, categorically imperative since it has no alternative but an immoral one, i.e., to lie. But if a maxim passes the test, it does not generally follow that it is categorically imperative, for its opposite may also pass the test, unlike the lying promise. For example, the maxim that I follow in driving on the right hand side of the road is universalizable; my driving in this manner is consistent with a world in which everyone did likewise. It does not follow that it is a categorical imperative that everyone drive on the right, for left side driving is (for example) equally universalizable. The test shows that right side driving is not immoral; it does not further show it mandatory. Kant's test is a negative one, not a positive one. It provides a quite general moral framework within which infinite variations of custom and manners are possible.[30]

Kant in fact distinguishes *morality*, i.e., the realm of obligations (e.g. promises) which are categorical, thus independent of my wants, momentary inclinations or happiness, from *prudence*, i.e., the realm of things promoting my happiness or welfare.[31] Within the bounds of morality, infinite variations are possible regarding prudence, since people conceive their happiness in different ways, happiness being, as Kant said, an ideal of the imagination.[32] What is categorical, for Kant, is therefore not the particular fabric of anyone's customs or culture in general but rather the imperative to conceive everyone as equally subject to any rules serving as maxims of action, the demand to treat everyone with the respect due every person, the injunction to regard everyone as an end in his own right and not merely as a means to the ends of others, to recognize in every other person the same self-governing legislative capacity that I claim for myself. Kant regards such capacity as the core of human dignity, which he holds to be beyond all price, being the basis for any other value that human beings may create or embody.[33]

Kant has suffered from the charges of critics that his view is too austere, too unbending. But what he vigorously excludes is contempt for persons, the treatment of persons as objects, or mere instruments, the unequal application of laws and rules, the blindness to the capacity that others have of legislating principles for themselves, the self-love or fear that leads people to make exceptions for themselves in the principles they claim to profess. Within this framework his view is actually hospitable to all sorts of variation, as we have seen above.

Kant wrote two centuries ago, and we have learned many things about cultural variation since his day. Not only have psychology, history and the social sciences of anthropology, sociology and linguistics been developed in their modern forms, but also philosophical investigations of moral issues and critical discussions of Kant's own views have proliferated, with the result that our intellectual landscape is substantially different from that of Kant's day. Yet his powerful moral vision continues to provide us with guidance under the circumstances of the present.

For as we have learned more and more about human diversity we have also learned more and more about human commonalities. Some of these commonalities we have outlined in the last section, as emerging out of the human capacity for action, made possible by symbolic function. And these commonalities do not fundamentally contradict but rather enrich Kant's conception of persons as beings capable of formulating varied maxims for their own conduct, ordering their acts to achieve goals, under the guidance of rules. Furthermore, the world has in the last two centuries gotten smaller and smaller, and the capacities for devastating conflicts greater and greater. How much more urgent it is for us, with the future increasingly foreshortened, to develop worldwide conceptions of our own mutuality, equality and reciprocity of position, to foster human dignity and respect for persons as basic attitudes within which all sorts of diversity in other respects may flourish.

Kant's view of society, as a kingdom of ends[34] within which free and rational beings would acknowledge such mutuality of freedom and incorporate one another's aims, where not immoral, into their own, may strike us now as hopelessly naive and unrealistic. But he was not predicting; he was formulating an ideal for human beings to strive for, their dignity contingent not on success in such striving but on their investing their action and effort in pursuits worthy of free and autonomously moral beings. The general outlines of such a vision as Kant's still seem to us to point the way in defining a goal for education in a global society of many cultures destined to share a shrinking world.

In the normative outlook of our project, at any rate, we have taken such a view. The common nature of human beings as intentional, norm-creating agents commands a fundamental respect. Human dignity is to be recognized and prized across whatever diversities divide us, and respect for persons takes a primary place among the values we espouse in thinking about education and society. Such a position does not amount to cultural relativism; we recognize that cultures themselves may differ with respect to how they honor these values. While the task of our project is not to issue moral verdicts and pass judgment on cultures of the past or the present, we have nevertheless, in organizing our data and concepts, taken the values outlined as basic assumptions and considered educational decision and policy as properly oriented to promote such values.

Moreover, in attempting to integrate scientific investigations in support of educational practice, we believe our normative assumptions give a special perspective on science itself. Too often science is viewed as a cold calculating machine, bloodless and value-less.[35] We believe science is better regarded as a common human effort to understand the circumstances in which we all, across the globe, find ourselves. Among these circumstances are our own cultural and historical diversities. To inquire into these differences of belief and purpose is to create a new layer of conversation across the barriers created by these very differences. Science is not a panacea, nor is it a worldwide culture in the full-bodied sense of the word. We consider it a universal conversation in the making, an intentional creation of a common symbolic scheme supplementing whatever other schemes already operate within us. Efforts to build cooperative studies across differences of culture are, at any rate, consistent with such a view. The human sciences are not to be thought of as somehow above and beyond their own subject matter, human action. We have conceived them as organized to advance the understanding of action and therefore value. In this effort, science has its own special value in helping to build, and not only study, the potential for a common human culture.

II

POTENTIAL: A CONCEPTUAL FRAMEWORK

A. INTRODUCTION

The picture we have painted of human nature is centered on the notion of action as *purposive*, *symbolic*, and *social* – action both reflective of prior norms and creative of new ones through the instrumentality of choice. Human lives thus do not ride on fixed rails; they do not follow trajectories already laid down by physics supplemented with biology. Their courses are modified by belief and interpretation, fear and hope, recollection and anticipation, symbolism and value. The newborn child, considered simply as a *biological unit*, is indeterminate as a *human being* – the texture of its life is still to be filled out largely by human effort, that is to say, by culture, history, education and decision.

Acknowledgment of such indeterminacy leads us to think of the dependent infant in relation to an array of imaginable or logically possible futures, of which the realization of some depends in good part upon what we do. What we do is, however, itself constrained by the particular child's enduring nature, which points in one direction rather than another. Among the child's merely imaginable, or logically possible futures, that is, we may deem some intrinsic to its nature and thus both valuable and empirically realizable, while judging others foreign to its nature and thus unrealizable. We tend then to categorize the former as its potentials, striving to realize them optimally. On the other hand, an abstractly valuable future we judge *at odds* with a child's nature – hence

41

beyond its empirical reach – is one we need expend no effort on, and can ignore with an easy conscience if not without regret.

The language of potential thus reflects distinctive features of human growth; it is also a device for discharging our educational responsibilities toward it. It is a tribute to the openness of the infant's future and the salience of human efforts in its development. It also advises us to choose for realization those conceivable futures intrinsic to children's natures (i.e. their potentials) ignoring the rest meanwhile.

Of course, even with such advice, much remains to be done: we need to determine what the potentials of a given child in fact are, and we need further to decide how most effectively to promote their realization. But the scope of our educational obligations is heavily circumscribed by the traditional language of potential. For we have imagined the child to have an enduring *nature*, and supposed certain of its logically possible futures to be intrinsic to such nature, hence invariable. Here is the *myth of fixed potentials*, already encountered in the last chapter. This myth spares us the worry over temporal variations in potential; the openness of the child's future is reduced to a set of possibilities unchanging over time. The *myth of harmonious potentials* spares us the worry over conflicts of realization requiring independent choice. Finally, the *myth of valuable potentials* spares us the worry over harmful or evil potentials requiring prevention rather than realization. Together, the three myths reduce the educational problem to a factual question: 'What potentials does the student have?', coupled with a technological question, 'How are these potentials most efficiently to be realized?'

B. PHILOSOPHICAL BACKGROUNDS

The myths we have criticized are the historical residues of the Aristotelian metaphysic of essences defining natural kinds. The properties intrinsic to the natural kind constitute its essence, at once defining the natural end of its members and explaining their development as progressive actualization of their ideal form; thus thought Aristotle. The acorn, potentially an oak, is moved by its potential oakhood toward realizing the final state comprising its natural end, the features of which define the essence of its species, and explain the growth stages of its members.[1]

The difficulties of this scheme, from a contemporary point of view, are notorious. The whole notion of species as fixed has been supplanted, through the rise of evolutionary theory, by the notion of species as alterable; the idea of a permanent nature with an enduring essence has simply been surrendered.[2] Independently of this shift in biological thinking, there are difficulties in understanding and applying the basic concepts. What is an essence anyway? An acorn is not only the seed of an oak but a morsel prized by squirrels. Why is the one property singled out as natural and explanatory, in preference to the other? Is the first more predictive than the second? But more acorns are eaten by squirrels than grow into oaks. True, if an acorn is properly nurtured, and protected from squirrels, etc., it will grow into an oak but, equally, if it is properly placed in the vicinity of hungry squirrels, it will, on the contrary, be eaten by a squirrel. Reference to *essential oakhood* will, in any case, not predict the outcome, and is thus of no use in explaining the acorn's development.[3]

Nor is it evident that essential properties, however conceived, yield moral recommendations or criteria of value. If the acorn's essence is to become an oak, this does not show it *ought* to become one; that the egg's essence is to become a chicken does not imply it is wrong to make an omelette. No magic bridge connects alleged *facts* concerning essences with the supposed *values* of their realizations. Were all these alleged facts accepted without argument, we should still face the necessity of deciding what to do in the face of them. In short, the concept of essence is itself unclear and untestable, its presupposition of the fixity of species incompatible with current science, and its alleged implication of value utterly spurious.

The background of the value implication is this: for Aristotle, the actual is better than the merely potential; to see is better than merely to have the power to see.[4] The perfectibility of human beings, in the tradition flowing from this doctrine, is a matter of actualizing the potentialities within them. This conception requires, however, a special view of evil.

Of any actual person – let us say, a repulsive bigot – it has to be said that in 'so far as he is actual he is perfect.' But what

43

of his bigotry? This, it is then necessary to argue, is not actual . . . the bigot does not actualize a human potentiality, he does not 'realize his nature,' by his bigotry. Rather, he fails to realize his nature, since he is deprived of some good which is potential in it. All potentialities, then, are for good. It is more than a little surprising how often perfectibilists have taken this for granted; the 'release of potentialities' is calmly identified with the release of potentialities *for good*.[5]

Transposed to education, the notion of actualizing the potential essential to persons becomes a criterion of value. Since, as suggested above, there is no clear criterion, in turn, of what is the potential essential to persons, we read our value predilections into such potential. Independently abhorring bigotry, we rule it out of the realm of potential; then we claim, circularly, that bigotry ought not to be developed since it is no part of the essence defining human potential.

It is a tribute to the power of philosophical ideas that the Aristotelian scheme we have criticized still holds enormous, if largely unconscious, sway over educational thought. (The point is illustrated in Chapter III, Section E, below.) Yet the notion of potential in education is subject to familiar difficulties of the sort we have set forth above. What *is* the criterion for judging that a given feature is *intrinsic* to a child's nature? Assuming we judge some feature to be intrinsic, how does that explain how the child actually develops? How does the idea of an intrinsic nature account for the flexibility and change characteristic of actual personal development? And why does the purportedly intrinsic character of a feature show that it is valuable? In practice, as we have seen, the value of potentialities is in fact presupposed as an additional premise. The notion that if only we had a scientific method for finding the *facts* about potential, we would then have a guide for *value judgment* is thus a notion that has to be given up. Yet scientists and educators, typically unaware of the philosophical backgrounds of their thought, continue to employ this notion and to apply it in practice.

C. RECONSTRUCTIONS OF POTENTIAL

The pitfalls of the traditional idea of potential should by now be evident. Used explicitly or tacitly presupposed in educational theory and social planning, the notions of intrinsic natures, fixed potentials, or essential talents offer untestable devices for projecting a limited and rigid view of human possibilities. They hold out the will-o'-the-wisp of a neutral science by which our social values can be determined without our need to take moral responsibility; and they offer meanwhile a convenient screen by which we can mask our value choices not only from others but even from ourselves.

Despite these criticisms, we may nevertheless strive to reconstruct the traditional language of potential so as to free it of the older troubles while retaining its practical applicability in educational contexts. The reconstruction in question is, in effect, replacement: new conceptualizations to substitute for the old. In the remainder of this chapter, we in fact set forth three reconstructed concepts of potential, a *capacity* notion, a *propensity* notion, and a *capability* notion. Our hope is that these three notions may be applied in a testable manner, free of covert value implications and metaphysical essentialism, that they may be compatible with the facts of developmental change in various social circumstances, and that they may prove useful in clarifying educational choice. We begin the task of reconstruction with some general observations.

In ordinary uses of the language of potential in education, we refer, not to existing or manifest capacities, skills, or other traits that a person may have, but rather to the possible future learning or development or acquisition of such features. To say of John that he is now a *pianist* (or, explicitly, that he can now play the piano) ascribes to him now the capacity or ability to play. On the other hand, to say of John that he is now a *potential pianist* does not imply that he now has the ability or capacity to play. Indeed, it implies that he *cannot* now play; to describe a concert pianist as having the capacity to play may be an understatement, while to describe him as a potential pianist would be an insult. But if the statement that John is now a potential pianist implies that he cannot now play, it assuredly says something more as well. What else, then, can be implied? Presumably, that he has the 'makings'

45

of a pianist, that he might be a pianist in the future. But what exactly does this mean?

It seems to be a sensible assertion, surely. For, of all those people who cannot now play the piano, some differ from the rest in being potential pianists. It is not sufficient for being a potential pianist to be merely unable to play. What more, then, is required; what distinguishes the potential pianists from the rest? To suppose that there is some essence of piano playing that they alone possess, some occult seed of piano talent now germinating inside them, or a ghostly pianist already performing inside their heads, or fingers, is sheer nonsense.

Perhaps, then, we are predicting of the potential pianists that they will acquire the ability to play at some time in the future, while those others who are not potential pianists will not. This is, at any rate, a clear distinction, but it is not the one we seek. For John may be a potential pianist and never in fact become a pianist at any time in the future. It is perfectly consistent to speak of unrealized potentials, to imagine that John's piano potential is, alas, never transformed into actual capacity. It follows that to ascribe a potential cannot be understood as predicting categorically that it will be realized.

If a potentiality-attribution is indeed a sensible assertion but neither ascribes an essence nor makes a categorical prediction, how exactly is its content to be construed? This is the basic conceptual problem to be faced. Unless we resolve this problem, we cannot hope to be clear about the issues that may be at stake in any apparent dispute over potential. Nor can we be clear about the evidence required to evaluate potential or the assumptions presupposed in claims to potential. We cannot, as a matter of fact, be sure there is any substance at all in such claims. Without a clarification of the meaning of the concept, the logic of its use must remain opaque.

D. POTENTIAL AS CAPACITY TO BECOME

Let us have another look at the notion of capacity. To say John is a potential pianist denies he has the capacity to play the piano, but says something more in addition. The problem is: what else? Our first proposal is that it says John has the *capacity to become a pianist*. He has now no *capacity to play* but he does now have another capacity, i.e. the *capacity to acquire the capacity to play* – to learn how to play, to develop into a player. We thus contrast the manifest capacity with the *capacity to achieve it*.

Of all those now lacking the manifest capacity, some now have the capacity to achieve it in the future, while others do not. Yet, even those having this capacity to achieve it in the future may or may not in fact do so: no categorical prediction of future realization is implied. We thus appear to have an interpretation of potential that meets the conditions earlier set. To attribute a potential under this interpretation neither ascribes an essence nor makes a categorical prediction, while it distinguishes some who lack the manifest capacity from others who also lack it. It becomes clear, moreover, why describing a concert pianist as a potential pianist is insulting. For under the present interpretation, to describe him thus is to say he has the capacity to *acquire* piano playing capacity and this in turn implies he does not already possess it: one cannot acquire what one already owns.

The underlying proposal can, moreover, be generalized. For we can apply it not only to the acquisition of capacities (such as playing the piano) but also to the acquisition of habits, traits, propensities and other characteristics. Thus, a person may be described as having the potential for understanding differential equations or as being a potentially heavy smoker, or as potentially a well-informed citizen, etc. Whatever the characteristic in question may be, the proposal under consideration interprets its *potential possession* at a given time as implying (1) its *manifest lack* at that time and asserting in addition (2) the *capacity to acquire* such characteristic at some time in the future. *Potentiality* is, in short, here taken as a sub-type of *capacity*, that is, the capacity to acquire a specified characteristic – to become someone possessing it.

This proposal rests, then, on the notion of capacity. But how is capacity itself to be interpreted? What does it mean to say of someone that he *can*, in fact, play the piano, or swim, or type, or ride a bicycle? Such expressions may, to be sure, carry different interpretations in different contexts. Here, the proposal we are concerned with takes one such interpretation as operative: it takes capacity as a sort of *possibility*, itself the denial of a necessity or *constraint*. Accordingly, to say it is possible that such-and-such is to say it is not necessary that *not* such-and-such. To say John can, i.e. it is possible that he will, play the piano, is to say it is not a foregone conclusion that he will not. In general, to affirm the capacity for a certain outcome is frequently just to deny that the outcome in question will assuredly not occur.[6]

Skilled performances, for example, require the coordination of several factors beyond the mere decision to perform. They require, for example, a permissive environment, appropriate means, minimal know-how. If any required factor is missing, the performance will be *prevented*. If we know such a factor is absent, we have good reason to suppose that the performance *will not* take place – because it *cannot*. Any one of a number of different preventive circumstances may block a given performance. I may say I can't drive today, knowing my car is in the repair shop; on another occasion, I may say I can't drive, since my arm is in a cast. Now, to negate the assertion that John *can't* drive is to say he *can*, that is, he has the *capacity* to drive. And this is in turn to deny that some relevant, allegedly preventive circumstance obtains, relevance being determined by the particular context. But, clearly, to assert that John *can* drive is not to predict that he *will*; it is only to deny the necessity that he *won't*.

Capacity, thus understood, denies the force of a putatively preventive factor salient in context. To say, after my engine has been repaired, that I am now able to drive again may amount to saying that a defective engine no longer prevents my driving. To say the very same thing after my broken arm has healed may rather be a way of indicating that my broken arm no longer prevents my driving; it would not normally be considered a refutation of my statement in the latter case to be told that my car had broken down again. Asserting a capacity serves here, then, to deny that some salient preventive circumstance obtains. It may, in other cases, concede the *existence* of the circumstances in question but deny that they are actually *preventive*: Of course Mary can ride a bike; the fact that she hasn't practiced for years does not prevent her riding. Generally speaking, to assert a *capacity* for such and such rebuts a presupposed argument for the *necessity* of not such and such, understood in context. The rebuttal may deny that the circumstances deemed preventive actually obtain in this case, or it may deny that such circumstances are in fact preventive. In any event, the capacity attribution rebuts an argument for the contrary constraint, perceived as salient in context.

Now the *acquisition* of a skill or a trait, no less than a skilled performance itself, is also preventable by a variety of circumstances. Such acquisition also depends on the coordination of several factors, the absence of any of which will provide adequate reason to suppose the acquisition will be blocked. No less than *driving* itself, *learning to drive* may be prevented by any of a variety of circumstances. To *deny* that a putatively preventive circumstance, relevant in context, obtains is thus to *affirm* the capacity for learning to drive, the capacity to acquire driving skill – to become a driver. And this, according to the proposal we have been considering, is what it means to say that someone is a *potential* driver.

Like affirmation of *capacity* in general, as we have explained it, affirmation of *potential* is contextual in its import. That is to say, some circumstance deemed preventive of learning to drive, and salient in context for whatever reason, is denied to obtain or to impede, by the attribution of potential in question. The focus of such attribution is the question whether the allegedly preventive circumstance uppermost in people's minds in the relevant context both impedes and obtains in the present case; a positive attribution implies that it does not.

The study of potential takes on a special interpretation under our foregoing, first proposal. It is not the search after occult essences, drives, or entelechies. It investigates the *capacity for acquisition* of features of various sorts and this, in turn, involves inquiry into the factors that may *impede* acquisition. The study of potential is, in effect, the study of conditions that block learning, prevent development, necessitate failure to attain some designated outcome. It is also the study of how such preventive circumstances may be instituted or themselves prevented in particular cases.

To investigate potential is thus, for example, to investigate such biologically preventive factors impeding desirable forms of learning as nutritional deficiencies, sensory or motor deprivation, damage to the nervous system, birth defects; it equally concerns prevention of undesirable outcomes, e.g. through nutritional therapy to block certain diseases. It is also to inquire into cultural factors that are preventive for learning, in particular, belief systems, institutions and policies that may impede acquisition. An important general point of interest is that *false* beliefs about preventive circumstances for a given trait may themselves become

49

preventive for that trait. A false belief that women cannot, for reasons of physiology, acquire mechanical skills may itself become a circumstance blocking such acquisition, especially when enshrined in policy and in social and educational institutions.

Under the present interpretation, the issue at stake when attribution or denial of a given potential is in dispute is whether or not the relevant acquisition is ruled out, given the factual circumstances. The issue is indeterminate unless it is made clear *which* circumstances are claimed, explicitly or implicitly, to be preventive of the acquisition in question. Given such clarification, the issue can, in theory, be resolved by determining (1) whether these circumstances do in fact obtain, and (2) whether or not such circumstances are, in general, preventive of the acquisition under discussion.

Attribution or denial of potential is not the only issue of importance; we are also concerned with *changes* in existing potentials. Such changes may, in certain cases, be brought about by deliberate effort; they are sometimes accessible to policy decision. That a given biological factor, for example, a neurological defect or other disability, blocks a given bit of desirable learning may be the case only if policy restricts therapy or ameliorative technology in certain ways. That a given cultural factor, for example, the level of available schooling, prevents certain learning outcomes may be true, but this level itself is typically alterable by policy decision.

The attribution or denial of potential is normally relative to certain presumptions as to the type of society taken as context, and, in particular, as to the policies in place. Relative to a certain degree of social effort, for example, it may be true to say that certain children cannot satisfy a given criterion of achievement. To state such a fact as if it implied some intrinsic lack in the children is, however, quite misleading. For it may also be true that the lack might be eliminated by a heightened social effort, *enhancing* their earlier potential.

Conversely, the possession of a given potential may later be *eliminated* by policy. Immunization against various diseases prevents their contraction by children, thus destroying undesirable potentials possessed earlier. Accessibility to policy decision depends, of course, upon the state of knowledge available; immunization against polio awaited the development of a suitable vaccine and was not a policy option prior to such development.

50

It must not be supposed that policy, itself a matter of cultural effort, is therefore germane only to cultural factors and powerless against the hard facts of biology. Biological factors may be tamed by knowledgeable policy, as witness the example of disease control. By contrast, cultural factors may be recalcitrant, deeply ingrained attitudes proving impervious to policy initiatives. Policy may attempt change in such cases over the long run, and may, even in the short run, moderate or alter traditional forms, but it may be powerless to change them fundamentally. The effective range of policy varies with knowledge. We cannot now say what forms of enhancement, or shrinkage of potential, future studies may make possible. Recognizing present limits is compatible with avoiding dogmatism about the future.

We now summarize the main points of this section. First of all, potential may be understood as a subtype of capacity – the capacity to become a being with certain characteristics, to acquire a feature of some sort. Second, attribution of potential, thus understood, refers explicitly or implicitly to features comprising some designated outcome. Third, the outcome in question may be deemed good or bad, desirable or not. A desirable outcome, thought of as a target state, is one we are disposed to render possible – one whose preventive conditions we wish to overcome or mitigate. An undesirable outcome is one we should like to preclude; our target states here are certain conditions blocking such outcome.

Fourth, potentials are in no case to be thought of as essences intrinsic to the person or as fixed and durable. The issue of potential is whether or not some features of the subject obtaining at the time in question, and relevant in context, indeed block the designated outcome. Fifth, attributions of potential and projected changes of potential reflect the state of knowledge, and the social context and policies, presumed by those making the attributions. With additional knowledge available, or an altered allocation of effort assumed, the picture of potential and its prospects may change in quite radical fashion. We have here what might be called a 'principle of relativity' of potential. Such relativity must always be borne in mind.

E. POTENTIAL AS PROPENSITY TO BECOME

A potentiality-attribution, we have said, denies an argument that a person *cannot* acquire some characteristic. But it makes no prediction that he *will* acquire it. Sometimes, however, a potentiality-attribution says more than just that a given outcome is *not ruled out*. It appears in fact to be saying something predictive on its own, rather than simply negating the contrary prediction. But it stops short of a categorical forecast of the outcome.

To say that Jones is a potential heart attack victim does not simply deny that some circumstance, generally precluding heart attacks, rules out an attack in his case. Nor, however, does it predict that Jones will in fact be a heart attack victim. It denies that Jones is now having an attack but it says something more – something stronger than the assertion of a mere capacity for an attack, but weaker than a categorical prediction of one.

Analogously, to describe John as potentially a heavy smoker says more than that some salient impediment does not preclude his becoming a heavy smoker, yet less than that he will indeed become one. And to say that he has the potential for understanding quantum theory or that he is a potential pianist often requires similar interpretation: it is not, in such cases, being asserted that he will in fact understand quantum theory – or be a pianist – but neither is it being said merely that such outcomes as these are not precluded. How then are such claims of 'intermediate strength' to be understood?

A clue is suggested by consideration of tendencies or propensities to certain sorts of voluntary behavior. When we say, in ordinary discourse, that someone has a tendency or propensity, rather than just a capacity, to swim, we say more than that his swimming is not prevented by some circumstance understood in context. But we make no categorical prediction of swimming either. What we often do is to make a certain sort of conditional prediction: *if* he has the chance *and* his choice is not constrained, he is likely to swim. A person who never swims under such conditions may yet have the capacity, but he could hardly be said to have the corresponding propensity. The ordinary propensity-attribution, while it does not categorically predict someone's swimming, in effect often characterizes him as being set to choose to swim, hence as likely to swim when he has the chance, unless his choice is interfered with. An ordinary propensity-attribution, in short, frequently tells us what a person is likely to do under conditions of opportunity and freedom of choice. It tells us something about his motivation.[7]

Now the general concept of *conditional prediction* may be detached from the motivational aspect and applied to our present problem. We do *not*, thus, suppose that a potential heart attack victim is set to choose an attack when he has the opportunity, or that a potential pianist is one who will in fact become a pianist unless his choice is interfered with or blocked. We no longer restrict ourselves just to those conditions – i.e. opportunity and free choice – involved in our example of swimming and similar cases. The general idea is simply that the outcome is predicted conditionally: it is not merely asserted to be *possible*, nor is it *flatly predicted*. Rather, it is predicted *if*, aside from there being no positive impediment, certain more or less vaguely specified conditions hold. This idea thus yields claims of just the 'intermediate strength' we have been seeking. If John is potentially a heavy smoker, he will become one *if* _____; to say he is a potential pianist is to convey that he will become one *if* _____.

The idea behind our second proposal is then to take the generalized notion of *propensity for acquisition*, as explained above, as a model for certain potentiality assertions, as we earlier took *capacity for acquisition* as the basis for certain others. A potentiality-attribution, for our second proposal, is thus to be understood as predicting some acquisition under conditions stated or implicit in context.

Sometimes the point of such attribution is cautionary. A potential heart attack victim is one who, as we might say, is likely to have a heart attack, *if* he does not mend his ways. Although unable to predict that he *will* have a heart attack, we may be able to judge that, given the evidence about his present condition, he is likely to have one unless certain changes take place. In other words, he will (with a certain probability) have an attack *if* prevailing conditions persist; he is 'at risk' of an attack. Such a cautionary message may of course be made more precise by giving a numerical estimate of the probability in question, by fixing the critical danger period of a probable attack, and by specifying the characteristics upon which the prediction is based.

We do not, in typical circumstances, similarly speak of a child as 'at risk' of becoming a pianist, although we may well describe him or her as a *potential pianist*. Such a description does not warn us that if steps are not taken to alter prevailing conditions, the child will turn out to be a pianist. But that is because we normally value acquiring the skills of a pianist as an outcome, rather than dreading and seeking to avert it, as we do a heart attack. Howard Gardner has suggested that we might in such cases speak of a person as being 'at promise' for the valued outcome in question. The point, in either case, is to affirm a conditional prediction. We convey, for example, that with a certain degree of effort, education, encouragement, or support, the child is likely to acquire the ability to play the piano. Conditional predictions of this sort are often imprecise because the relevant conditions are not sufficiently spelled out. But understanding certain potentiality-attributions *as* conditional predictions enables us to see what claims are implicit and to evaluate their determinacy and persuasiveness. It also enables us to see how they might be made more precise by further investigation.

Often, the force of a potentiality-attribution is *comparative* rather than *categorical*. Robert may thus be said to have *greater* potentiality for heart attack than Richard because a greater modification of his circumstances than of Richard's is required in order that the likelihood of an attack for both be reduced to the same level. Or, if both likelihoods are the same, Richard's potentiality may be said to be smaller than Robert's in that less effort is required to keep Richard's likelihood at the reduced level. Jane may be said to have greater potential for the piano than Eileen in that, for the same level of effort or instruction, Jane is predicted to attain a higher degree of proficiency in playing the instrument, during a fixed period of time. Or the claim may rather be that, whereas both reach a fixed level of proficiency with the same level of effort, Jane is likely to take a shorter time to get there or, conversely, to require less effort to match Eileen's level in a fixed time interval. In all such cases, the common element remains that the potentiality-attribution makes a prediction only *relative to* conditions to be understood in context.

Now conditional predictions may be linked together to form sequential chains. Such chains enable us to interpret the psychologically important concept of development. A given chain may tell us that, under initially assumed conditions, a certain stage is likely to come about which, if additional conditions may be assumed at that time, is likely to be followed by a further stage, and so on, until a designated outcome or a target state is reached.

The need to stretch the prediction out over a series of stages arises because we may be in no position to predict the target state from initial conditions alone. However, we may be able to provide a conditional prediction extending from initial conditions to an intermediate state. Then, given such state plus the assumption of further concurrent conditions, we may be able to predict the target itself conditionally. In similar fashion, any number of intermediate states may theoretically be linked together to form a sequential chain. Thus, from the person X's initial state S_1 and assumed laws L_1 we predict intermediate state S_2; from S_2 plus simultaneous further conditions C_2 and laws L_2 we predict S_3 etc., and from S_{n-1}, plus simultaneous conditions C_{n-1} and L_{n-1}, we predict the target state S_n.[8]

It is important not to confuse such a chain with another sort of linkage, yielding what might be called the 'domino theory of prediction.' An example is that of an oil leak in an engine, which causes the engine to stall: because of the leak, the oil will drain out, depriving pistons and cylinders of lubrication, thus producing frictional heating and expansion of piston and cylinder walls, so that metals will lock tightly and the engine will stop.[9] In this case the sequence of sub-laws covering what happens between oil leak and engine stall logically implies the global law connecting the first stage (oil leak) directly to the last (stalled engine) within the constant environment presupposed. Given the oil leak, the stall may thus be predicted from it alone, assuming only the general constancy of the local environment, the so-called 'boundary conditions.'

The more typical case by far is of the sort we have previously considered, in which there is no such global law connecting the first and the final stage within constant boundary conditions. Rather, each transitional stage requires additional simultaneous conditions in order to enable prediction of the ensuing stage. This is, in effect, an *interactionist* picture, in which the initial stage does not itself warrant prediction of the final outcome, within constant boundary conditions. Rather, for the outcome to be predicted, a number of appropriate 'ifs,' characterizing the environment at intermediate times, have also to be realized.

There are differences in the degree to which we count on the infusion of relevant intermediate conditions in given cases. Where these infusions are precarious, the 'interactionism' of the schema is salient. Where we are, however, fairly confident in counting on them, the interactionism recedes from our attention, and the picture may approximate the domino image for practical purposes. Theoretically, however, the interaction remains as firm as ever, for the timed cooperation of suitable conditions is required to move each link forward to the next, no matter how much we may take such conditions for granted.

These timed conditions vary, as well, in the degree to which they are subject to our control. Obviously, this feature affects the extent to which the process of development is pictured as moving forward under its own power with no help from us or, alternatively, as requiring active intervention. Education construed as development has, perhaps typically, been taken to require the exercise of *restraint* by educators, at other times to require their active participation and control of the process.

Now to study potential, under the present interpretation, is to study the bases of conditional predictions of the acquisition of various features. In typically interesting cases, it is to study chained sequential predictions relating to educational development. What laws are available for predicting the intermediate and target states S referred to in our schematic account of five paragraphs above? What sorts of persons X and conditions C are presupposed in applying such laws, if any? What target outcomes are selected as being most desirable to promote; what outcomes most desirable to avoid? Where empirical information is currently inadequate to determine relevant developmental chains, what research seems most likely to help fill out the sequential schema?

As before, we note the importance of studying conditions of a biological as well as a cultural sort. And, as before, we emphasize that the beliefs and expectations of the subject X as well as of others relating to X may themselves constitute significant factors, whether true or false, realistic or not. This fact is illustrated not only by the importance of the pupil's own attitude in and toward learning, but also by the significance of the attitudes of others – in particular, parents and teachers – toward the pupil.

The term 'development' typically carries with it connotations of value; the word suggests changes from lesser to greater organization or adequacy or comprehensiveness. Thus, simply to label a set of changes an instance of 'development' frequently conveys the judgment that it leads from a less desirable to a more desirable state. It is important to note that no such connotation is attached to the interpretation of development offered in connection with our present proposal. The general notion of changes predictable by law from earlier changes plus auxiliary conditions implies nothing as to the relative value or adequacy of the initial and terminal states in question. Under the interpretation here suggested, there are developments we may judge desirable and others we may judge undesirable, some we wish to promote, others to forestall.

Indeed, we may now begin our summary of the present section by elaborating this aspect. The conditional predictions that underlie our second proposal make of potential a subtype of propensity – the propensity to become *something or other*, or to acquire a feature of *a certain sort*, with no value restrictions presupposed. We must not imagine a unique line of development emanating from any initial state, but rather picture any number of such lines radiating in all directions from the starting state toward end-points both desirable and not. Second, any attribution of potential of course makes reference, explicit or implicit, to some outcome, whatever its value may be deemed to be. Third, such attribution may be followed by an attempt at realization but it may also be cautionary – alerting to outcomes to be avoided, if at all possible.

Fourth, potentials, pointing to conditionally predictable end-points traceable from initial states, are of course not to be thought of as essences – immanent goals of the subject, explaining the course of changes from such initial states to these end-points. For what is conditionally predictable from the subject's starting-point, plus auxiliary conditions possibly occurring along the way, can by no means be attributed to him as a *goal*, under the most liberal assignment of goals. Nor, since there is no single privileged end-point but an indefinitely large number hypothetically accessible from any beginning state – most remaining unrealized anyhow – does it make sense to think of them as explanatory.

Fifth, potentials understood as propensities can hardly be considered intrinsic to the subject. The cooperation of contextual circumstances is presupposed, most strikingly in the chained

57

developmental sequences we have discussed. These sequences, moreover, have to be discovered, and they depend in the normal case on policies and resource allocations assumed in effect. Attributions of potential thus reflect the attributor's state of knowledge and the values and policies he presumes as part of the social context. This same point was mentioned in connection with our first proposal and we referred to it there as a principle of the relativity of potential. Such relativity applies here equally.

F. POTENTIAL AS CAPABILITY TO BECOME

We turn now to a third reconstruction of potential, one that hinges on the agent's *capability*, that is, his effectiveness in promoting a designated outcome. Consider, for example, a skilled performer in an environment which is permissive, i.e. which does not prevent the performance in question. Beyond the *capacity* to perform, the skilled performer also has *capability*. He can be generally *relied on* to perform properly under these conditions, *if* he chooses to. A less skilled performer is distinguishable by a lower degree of reliability in producing proper performances at will, under similar conditions. Thus, two archers of unequal skill show differing reliability in hitting the target, under the same environmental circumstances, when they are both in fact *trying* to hit the target. Greater skill is exhibited neither in greater environmental capacity nor in a higher frequency of hits *in general*. Such higher frequency is significant only when both archers, in similarly permissive environments, are striving to hit the target.

The factor of skill, or more generally *capability*, brings the performance, or other designated outcome, within the power or control of the agent – within the range of his or her intent or decision. To the degree that a person is capable, then – assuming no positive prevention of a contextually relevant sort – if he decides to produce the outcome in question, he is likely to do so. Capability thus authorizes a special kind of conditional prediction, one in which the person's own decision or effort enables us to predict the outcome with a fair degree of confidence.

This sort of conditional prediction (as well as the associated notion of development it engenders) places the agent's own initiative or striving at the center of consideration, rather than supposing him to be simply a passive recipient of external influences playing upon him. Enhancement of the agent's capability increases the effectiveness of his efforts and so, in one clear sense, his freedom of action. If he lacks the capability of hitting the target, his trying is ineffective – he cannot effectively choose to hit it, even under permissive circumstances. With the capability, this choice opens up realistically for the first time, and with it a new access of freedom. He is *empowered* to hit the target.

The concept of capability, as here interpreted, has been dealt with variously in recent philosophical writings. Perhaps it has most frequently been associated with G. E. Moore's discussion of free will as a matter of what I *could* have done – itself in turn a matter of what I *should* have done *if* I had chosen. I *could*, said Moore, have walked a mile in twenty minutes this morning (though I did not), but I certainly *could not* have run two miles in five minutes this morning (and of course I did not). Wherein lies the difference, in view of the fact that neither possibility was in fact realized? The difference, says Moore, is that *if* I had chosen to walk a mile in twenty minutes this morning, I should have, but even if I had chosen to run two miles in five minutes yesterday, I should not have. The difference, one might say, lies in the relative effectiveness of the choice in question to bring about the object of choice.[10]

Now this concept has sometimes been taken itself as *capacity*, but we have already reserved the term 'capacity' for other uses. Thus we refer to the present notion as *capability*, recognizing that this term is employed in various other ways by other writers. Capability, as we use it here, is a notion linked to that of freedom, offering, along Moore's lines, an account of one sense of that ambiguous and difficult term. Whether it offers a complete interpretation of freedom of the will or not is a point of philosophical controversy on which we need not here take sides. It will be enough for our purpose to fix the concept of *capability* as embracing what comes within the range of a person's effective choice, effort or decision – what it is in a person's *power* to do and what, in that sense, he is effectively free to do.

To enhance an agent's capability to perform is to empower him to perform. For it is to bring it about that his performance will ensue upon his decision or effort, given favorable circumstances, i.e. no salient environmental impediment. Now it is important to see the difference between such enhancement of capability and the enhancement of capacity – the difference between empowering the agent to perform and what we might refer to as enabling him to perform.

To enhance capacity, thus (in our terminology) enabling the agent to perform is to overcome some contextually salient preventive circumstance blocking the performance. To enable John to drive is to remove some such condition impeding his driving, consequently making such driving possible. With the impediment removed, we are, however, in no position to infer that John *will* drive, nor can we infer that, in general, if he makes the effort, he will. It is the latter property that constitutes capability rather than capacity and that differentiates empowering from mere enabling.

It is important to note that even if lack of choice is itself taken as the relevant impediment, removing it does not yield capability. Assume that if John does not choose to swim he certainly will not swim; it does not follow that if he does choose, he will swim. Getting John in fact to choose to swim may be to remove the particular impediment to swimming relevant in context. But such enabling does not suffice to yield capability – to warrant that John will swim if he chooses. Removing the impediment eliminates John's guaranteed failure; it does not establish his guaranteed, or even likely, success. Thus empowering goes beyond enabling.

Normally, impediments are construed not as *including* lack of choice, but as constituting constraints *on* choice. Encouraging choice is then identified with the process of *motivation* rather than enabling. Motivation, so understood, is independent of empowering, which does not necessarily promote a positive attitude toward the performance in question. Though empowering goes beyond enabling, neither warrants the conclusion that the subject likes or values the performance in question.

To enable Jane to swim is to remove some basis for predicting she won't swim. To empower her to swim is to bring it about that if she decides to swim, then, under permissive conditions, she will – i.e. she can be predicted to swim if not interfered with, given that she chooses to. She may, however, be empowered as well as enabled but still dislike swimming and so regularly avoid it. To get her to value swimming is, further, to bring it about that she will in fact choose to and thus that she will, unless interfered with, indeed swim. It is to promote what, in the *ordinary* sense of the term, is her propensity to swim. Empowering, however, stops short of the promotion of positive valuation of the performance in question; it creates the capability, skill or power, leaving the matter of valuation, exercise or decision open.

We now apply the concept of capability to *potential*. To say that someone has the potential for being an athlete is, under the present, third proposal, to say he has the *capability to become* one, that is, that he can be predicted to become one if he makes the effort to. We are, more generally, concerned with the acquisition of a feature of one or another sort. As we took *capacity for acquisition* to be the basis of our first interpretation above, and *propensity for acquisition* to be the basis of our second interpretation, we here take *capability for acquisition* as the basis of our third interpretation of potential.

To say someone has the capability to acquire a given feature thus means he will if he tries, under non-interfering conditions. That is, it is up to him whether he acquires the feature in question; he has the power, the means, the skill to choose effectively to acquire such a feature. A student's potential to be an athlete, a mathematician, a musician or a carpenter is his capability to learn what is needed to become one. If he has this capability, it is within the effective range of his decision whether or not he acquires the feature in question. To gauge X's potential for a given feature is, under this third interpretation, to judge whether (given permissive circumstances) his effort would be effective in making its acquisition likely.

Now to increase or enhance potential, under the present interpretation, is to empower the person to acquire the feature in question or, more briefly, to empower the relevant learning. It puts the means of learning within the person's decision range, thus putting the learning itself within his effective grasp. Increasing a person's potential, in this sense, heightens the effectiveness of his learning efforts, increasing his powers of self-determination by putting his future dispositions within range of his own choice.

The study of potential, under our third proposal, is the study of empirical conditions of the capability to learn. What factors, in given social circumstances, account for individual variations in such potential for specified learning outcomes? How, in such circumstances, may potential be enhanced? That is, beyond the creation of permissive environments for learning, how may the student's *capability to learn* be strengthened? How is it weakened? What are the preconditions, biological and cultural, and what are the basic arts and skills of learning of various sorts that may contribute to the enhancement of worthwhile potentials? Such questions have to do with the effective use that might be made of opportunities provided – with the *capability* to exploit available *capacity*.

We now summarize our discussion of the present interpretation. Potential, first of all, is here taken as a subtype of capability i.e. the capability to acquire some feature or other. Thus, second, attributions of potential always refer to some hypothetical outcome. Third, this outcome may be considered good or bad, positive or negative in value. An outcome deemed valuable by us is one we may want to put within reach of the student's effective choice. An outcome deemed undesirable is one we may want to keep outside the range of such choice. Thus, we may want to increase the student's capability to become an athlete or a mathematician, but not a safecracker or a forger or drug addict. Capabilities are, however, so interwoven that such divisions are not, in general, possible. To empower the student to learn the arts of healing is at the same time to empower him to learn methods of poisoning. To keep the learning of poisoning out of his range of decision would also keep the learning of healing out of his range of decision. Capability is power of effective choice and such power does not follow the channels of value judgment that may be laid down for it.

Education thus supplements the enhancement of capability with attention to motivation, i.e. with provision of relevant information and initiation into some scheme of values. The physician is expected not to poison – and not because he lacks the capability (if he did he would be incompetent) but because his choices are governed by relevant information and appropriate values. To develop a student's capability to learn is, in general, to give him skills which may be employed for a variety of ends, both good and bad. With the development of his powers of effective choice goes responsibility for the exercise of such powers.

Fourth, potentials, construed as capabilities of acquisition are surely not intrinsic to the person; they may be developed or constricted over time. Finally, the principle of relativity of potential earlier mentioned holds here as well. For the effectiveness of a person's effort in learning depends heavily on the social and educational environment. Here, as before, attributions of potential reflect the attributor's state of knowledge and the context presupposed.

G. INTERRELATIONS OF THE THREE CONCEPTS OF POTENTIAL

What are the relations between the three concepts we have introduced? To begin with, they all share certain properties. Each is interpreted as having to do with the acquisition of a feature that is now manifestly absent. The designated feature may be thought to be good or bad, desirable or not, and such evaluations, by the subject and by others, may show considerable variation.

In no case is potential a metaphysical essence governing the predetermined direction of the subject's development, nor is it a durable feature intrinsic to the subject. It has been uniformly interpreted here as reflecting both the subject and his social environment, and, moreover, as open to considerable change. Finally, attributions of potential, in each of the versions we have distinguished, are subject to variation with the attributor's state of knowledge and presumptions as to the policics, resource allocations, and other aspects of the context in question.

Our interpretations radically alter traditional conceptions of potential. For none of our interpretations can it be the case that determining an agent's potentials automatically yields prescriptions for our treatment of him. To link ascriptions of potential with recommendations for action requires independent value assumptions. Nor can we categorically assert or deny potential of an agent as if it were a property of his own, in isolation from the context. Whether we ascribe potential or not depends in part on our presumptions about the social environment, inclusive of the policies in force.

Finally, each of our interpretations provides an analysis of what a potentiality-attribution is to mean. It requires certain conditions to be satisfied for such an attribution to be correct. Thus, it bars simple assertion or denial on the basis of an unanalyzed intuition as to the agent's nature. The information required as evidence by each interpretation must be supplied. If it is not available, it must at least be conceded to be relevant to potentiality-claims advanced. Accordingly, a test of such claims is in principle determinable, and disputes over them are, in theory, resolvable. Where relevant information is lacking, each interpretation, moreover, points to the sort of inquiries needed to fill out the sketchy picture.

Let us now see how our three concepts diverge. Referring to capacity, a potentiality-attribution denies a counter-necessity. *Which* counter-necessity – that is, which impediment to acquisition – must be gleaned from the context, for the attribution in itself does not normally state it. Underlying the question of capacity for acquisition is, then, the prior question of what may block acquisition – of what necessities are thought, in virtue of presumed general laws, to run counter to such acquisition, in circumstances believed to be those of the agent.

A capacity asserted, it does not follow that its object can be predicted. To deny a counter-necessity is not tantamount to asserting its parallel positive necessity. Assume that the fact I can swim means it is not necessary that I won't. It doesn't follow from this fact that necessarily I will. What then can be said about cases where the outcome is positively, if not categorically, predicted?

The propensity interpretation proposes conditional prediction as a basis for thinking about potential. The metaphysical idea of necessity is replaced by lawlike generalizations of an if-then character. Moreover, we can interpret courses of development in terms of chains of conditional predictions, leading from their initial states to their end states, respectively, given auxiliary assumptions at each juncture. Doubt is thus cast on the widespread tendency to think of development as following a unique course from the present into the future. The selection of any such course as canonical reveals assumptions of value.

Conditional prediction receives a specialization in the capability interpretation of potential. For here, the *if* which activates the if-then connection is, in particular, the agent's own choice. He potentially has a certain feature, not in the sense merely that its acquisition is not ruled out (capacity interpretation), nor even in the general sense that such acquisition can be positively predicted under certain conditions (propensity interpretation), but rather in the special sense that it can be predicted, given his effort. The acquisition in question is up to him. We are, in effect, here concerned not just with *development* but with *self-development*, the effectiveness of an agent's choice of his own future characteristics.

The three concepts we have introduced are compatible with one another. They are not to be thought of as in competition. They provide mutually supplementary analytic schemata for clarifying three important aspects of education and growth, viz. impediments to the acquisition of various features, conditions under which such acquisition may develop and circumstances in which agents may be empowered to develop, as they choose. In terms previously employed, the issues they pinpoint concern impediments to acquisition, conditional propensities to acquisition, and capabilities of acquisition. Or, finally, the *enabling* of learning, the *development* of learning, and *self*-development, or the *empowering* of learning.

In the last chapter, we stressed the importance of symbolism in human life; the role of choice, belief and value; the time-binding qualifying action; and the notions of self and community. In the present chapter, we have emphasized several related aspects. First of all, the social context of potential, under every one of our interpretations, was made plain – its interactional as distinct from its intrinsic character.

We have further emphasized the future reference of potentiality-attributions. We look at the agent not just as what he is, but as what he might become, as what under given conditions he is likely to become, or indeed as what, if he chooses, he will become. Our vision of the manifest characteristics of persons is strongly tempered by such future reference and the converse is also true; we judge their future characteristics in the light of their manifest features. Both directions of judgment are applicable to communities as well and both are influenced by our own memories of the past and of lessons we think we have learned from the past.

In every one of our interpretations, some designated outcome forms the focus of the potentiality-attribution. Whether we wish to promote realization of the outcome in question or the reverse depends on how we view it in respect of value. A potential that spurs some to promote realization may spur others to prevent such realization. Changing values are reflected in changing treatments of admitted potentials, as witness, for example, recent transformations in the social roles of men and women in the West. Young people often differ in this way from their elders in assessing the treatment to be accorded their own potentials. How such conflicts of evaluation are dealt with constitutes an important feature of any social organization.

We have seen that the beliefs of the attributor affect the potentiality-attribution. We have further noted that false beliefs may become preventive factors in their own right. Students may, in this way, wrongly believe that certain factors block their achievement of specified goals. Such belief may, however, itself block this achievement. The belief system of the subject must therefore always be taken into account in assessing his potentials.

In education this is critically important, since children do not have any way of assessing their own powers at the outset. They learn what they can do by absorbing the beliefs of their elders as to what they can do. The thrill of new mastery often springs from the confirmation of potential the child did not believe it had. Often too, such mastery is facilitated by the teacher's display of faith in the student's potential, which overcomes the student's groundless skepticism.

In thinking about potential we have dealt with choice. For we have discussed the evaluations attaching to potentials and their realizations – and evaluations imply the possibility of choice. We have mentioned that the subject of a potentiality-attribution may differ from others in evaluating the realizations in question and may thus differ from them fundamentally in how he regards his choices. But, further, the subject may not even believe he has the potential attributed to him by others. He may possibly lack the very means for symbolizing the realization in question. Thus he may not be able even to conceive the choices attributable to him by others. This is particularly striking in connection with potential as capability, where choice is an explicit ingredient. Consequently, the promise of self-development seen from the standpoint of the outsider may be invisible to the agent himself.[11]

When we speak of potential, we must always keep in mind the possibility of such disparities of vision. That is, we must avoid falling into the habit of thinking with the outsider, and neglecting the insider's vantage. A danger of what we may call the development frame of mind is the presumption that the developer's assessment is the critical one, that it is his state of knowledge, symbolism, and values that determine the potential of the subject. The developer and the policy maker play important roles, to be sure, and nothing here said denies this fact. What is being urged, rather, is that these roles themselves require sensitivity to the symbolic capacities, states of belief, feelings, and values of the agents whose potentials are being gauged. It is here that the themes of the previous chapter find their fundamental application.

III

THE FRAMEWORK APPLIED
AND ILLUSTRATED

A. INTRODUCTION

The purpose of the present chapter is to sketch some empirical applications of the reconstructed potentiality-concepts recently presented. Our aim is a strictly limited one: we do not pretend to summarize, or even to outline, what is known in any domain of research. We hope rather to show, through selected illustrations, drawn from biology, social science and education, how our analytical concepts may be employed in application to empirical materials. In pursuing this aim, our goal is to provide a more concrete understanding of these concepts than an abstract account alone can offer. Further, we hope to suggest the value of our framework both in interpreting significant results already available, and in guiding future research, reflection and practice.

It is important to note one basic point before we embark on our account of applications. The point is implicit in much of our discussion, but it is worth stating directly at this time, since our ensuing procedure may suggest that *only* empirical applicability may be deemed relevant to an evaluation of a conceptual framework. While such applicability is of course of major importance – and indeed of central concern in this chapter – we nevertheless do not hold it to be of *exclusive* relevance in assessing the import of an analytic scheme.

Such a scheme must, in addition, strive to bring philosophical clarity and system to the subject matter, define criteria for the deployment of basic descriptive terms, and explain what sorts of evidence or argument bear on the justification of relevant claims. In working toward these goals, a scheme in progress will, typically, not only incorporate results as given but will criticize, redefine, and reformulate such results from a systematic point of view. Further, it will tend to suggest the relation of empirical matters to considerations from which researchers often abstract in the course of their work, e.g. considerations of value. Finally, an analytical scheme will be judged as of higher merit to the degree it does not merely reflect past investigations but points out new directions for inquiry and suggests new questions for reflection.

From the point of view of those practically concerned with a particular empirical result, it is, moreover, of critical importance how the result is analytically formulated and systematically oriented. For it is this that determines how the result relates to other results, to future as well as past research, and to questions of meaning, value and purpose. The mere empirical applicability of a scheme must, then, be supplemented by judgment of its systematic import, in gauging its worth.

The importance of integrating research questions and philosophical considerations in the design of action programs has been emphasized in a recent review of such programs as follows:

> when any of our suppositions about behavioral development
> and ways of influencing it are translated into action programs
> in a developing country – for example the kind of work
> inspired by the 'Higher Horizons' compensatory notions –
> we are confronted with an even more confused mass of
> research questions than we are in Europe. But by no means
> all or even the most important questions are properly research
> questions. They touch upon ethical, philosophical and social
> issues. Such down-to-earth initial choices as, for example, are
> involved in the determination and specification of criteria of
> 'good' or 'adaptive' or 'optimal' or even 'desired' development
> and their embodiment in specific partial objectives – like
> enhanced verbal development, future orientation,
> achievement motivation, even social change by the efforts of
> the community itself – make the selection of samples, research
> designs and so on, not only difficult but absolutely critical
> particularly if we wish to respect cultural difference and
> pluralism.[1]

The writer goes on to urge 'sensitive exploration of the practical, philosophical and research implications of innovative work in changing cultures,' and concludes his discussion with a plea for extension of 'our field of interest into consideration of the philosophic aspects of our working concepts of evaluation, innovation and social change, which are heavy with ideological and value implications which we cannot ignore. We have to integrate them into our scientific thinking and research planning.' Such integration of philosophy, science and value in the context of action represents the large background against which the question of specific empirical applicability is to be viewed in the discussions to follow.

We shall organize the remainder of our discussion in this chapter around four illustrative topics, as follows: in the next section, we treat the capacity notion of potential, relating it to our first illustrative topic of *critical periods* and *plasticity* in biological development. In the following section, we discuss the propensity notion of potential, relating it to our second illustrative topic of *canalization*, or *central tendencies* in development, whether biological or psychological. Further, we relate the propensity notion to the third topic of *international development*. In the ensuing section, we relate the capability notion of potential to the fourth topic of *basic skills* in education. Together, our illustrations exemplify the several levels of our concern, biology, psychology, cross-cultural studies, and education. We hope to show how key concepts of our framework help us to interpret and to integrate materials drawn from these various levels. Finally, in a coda, we revisit the three myths of potential, illustrating some outcomes of the demythologizing process we have undertaken here.

B. CAPACITY AND PREVENTION

The capacity notion of potential, as we have seen, denies an impediment to acquisition of some characteristic by a person. An individual with a potential, thus understood, is one whose acquisition of the relevant feature is not blocked by a salient preventive circumstance. When the problem arises as to whether attribution of a certain potential is warranted or not, the issue is thus whether or not the allegedly preventive circumstance in question both impedes acquisition and indeed obtains in the relevant context.

As we have emphasized in the previous chapter, the systematic study of potential takes on a special interpretation, looked at in this way. It seeks to determine the factors that impede acquisition, the conditions that block learning, the circumstances that prevent development or necessitate failure to attain some target state. It is concerned also to inquire into ways in which such preventive conditions may themselves be prevented or, rather – as in the case of inoculations against serious diseases – in fact instituted, in particular cases.

We have mentioned, in the last chapter, the example of certain biological factors impeding desirable forms of learning; nutritional deficiencies, sensory or motor deprivation, damage to the nervous system, birth defects, infectious diseases of various sorts may thus be viewed as negations of desirable outcomes. To negate such negations in turn is to enhance or release the potentials for such outcomes, making forms of learning possible that are otherwise ruled out. Sometimes such enhancement is within the present reach of policy, that is, accessible to available social resources, within tolerable limits of cost and effort. Sometimes it is out of policy reach, but within the range of available technical knowledge. Where it eludes even such range, it may conceivably follow upon discoveries yet to be made; here is a critical point at which research may impinge on practice.

Now the negation of preventive circumstances requires further analysis. Recall the fact, stressed in our earlier discussions, that prevention is always presumed to take place within a given context: that a certain condition in fact constitutes an impediment is normally asserted only under the presumption that it obtains within a society of a certain sort, characterized by customs, purposes, and policies of certain kinds. That is, the condition in question impedes, *assuming* that certain auxiliary circumstances are in place. That a particular biological condition blocks a behavioral outcome may thus, in certain cases, be affirmed only on the tacit assumption that the relevant therapy or ameliorative devices are unavailable. The block is, in effect, characterized as a function not of the biological condition alone but of the condition plus the unavailability in question.

Accordingly, what we have termed the negation of a preventive circumstance may take roughly two forms: one is elimination of the *preventive circumstance* itself, the other is elimination rather of the relevant *auxiliary circumstances*, so that the preventive effect is no longer to be anticipated. A structural injury impeding the development of certain behavioral functions *under normal conditions* may thus be 'negated' through (i) avoidance of the injury itself or, failing avoidance, its healing or repair, or alternatively, (ii) alteration of presupposed normal conditions so that the injury, though persisting, ceases to signal impairment of the functions in question – such alteration consisting, for example, in provision of special training, or prostheses, or new problem-solving procedures. Research in both these directions is obviously of high importance, i.e. inquiry into ways of avoiding or erasing the putative impediment itself and, alternatively, inquiry into ways of removing its sting by altering auxiliary circumstances. Both sorts of inquiry are, as we have seen, investigations into the enhancement of potential.

Topic I Critical Periods and Plasticity

We shall now illustrate several of the foregoing themes by reference to the notion of *critical periods* in development, that is to say, periods during which some condition must obtain if specified functions are to be achieved; failure of the condition during the relevant interval, in other words, blocks acquisition of the functions in question. Now we have already encountered the general concept in our early discussion of the idea that certain educational moments must be caught or they are gone forever, destroying potentials previously available: educators thus generally hold that the growth of central dimensions of character and intellect, e.g. self-confidence, curiosity, is governed by critical temporal constraints. Our discussion also noted, however, that widely diverse areas of development exemplify such constraints as well, instancing chess, the violin and ballet, which need to be learned early if at all, and referring, too, to the visual system as maturing only within the bounds of relevant critical periods.

Here, we shall look more closely at the case of the visual system as exemplifying some of the basic concepts of our framework. Investigation of the developing visual system in mammals shows

72

that appropriate visual stimulation is required during certain periods if normal functions are to be attained. And this is to say, as we have seen, that the lack of such stimulation during the appropriate intervals *prevents* attainment of the functions in question.

Amblyopia, or dimness of vision, in particular, exemplifies the effect of a time-dependent impediment to the acquisition of normal visual function. An impairment that may result from visual disturbances early in life, amblyopia persists even after the original problem has been corrected and even though the retina seems normal, thus suggesting defect in the central nervous system. Amblyopia may be caused by an early deprivation of form vision due to a cataract or astigmatism that blocks or blurs vision, or by a strabismus, a misalignment of the eyes, in which the deviant eye cannot focus on an object concurrently with the normal eye.[2] In each case, a permanent reduction in the acuity of the deprived eye may result, and that eye tends to be suppressed by the good eye.

Amblyopia affects up to 6 per cent of sample populations of human beings. Efforts to study this condition have involved the experimental deprivation of vision in animals. Amblyopia has thus been induced in kittens and in monkeys, by suturing closed the eyelid of one eye early in the animal's life. When the sutured eyelid is opened following a period of deprivation, visually guided behavior seems normal when both eyes are in use. However, if the normal eye is now closed, and the animal forced to use only the deprived eye, the animal behaves as though it were blind and, although an improvement occurs over the following weeks, permanent behavioral deficits remain.[3] Now it is a striking fact that if cats undergo the same procedure *later in life*, no behavioral anomalies result.[4] The deprivation of vision has severe effects only if it occurs within the appropriate early period in the animal's life.

Early experience seems, in several cases, to play a role in developing neural systems, interacting, in such cases, with innate processes during sensitive periods of time. The relevant timetable of such periods varies from system to system and, even within systems, for different types of neurons. But the fact that, in at least certain systems (e.g. visual, auditory, bird song), appropriate levels of experiential input may be required during critical periods for the attainment of normal function, is not in doubt.[5]

73

Can deficits, once produced by relevant critical deprivations, be overcome? This question of *the reversibility of deficits*, or what has sometimes been termed the issue of plasticity, has been much debated but it is clear from our previous discussion that it cannot be profitably dealt with in the abstract, or in a categorical manner. First of all, that a crucial deprivation has occurred during a critical period and that attainment of normal function has therefore been blocked may mean only that it has been blocked *at the normally expected juncture*. Recuperation may in certain cases occur spontaneously at a later period, the capacity for such recuperation itself, however, likely to diminish with the age of the organism.[6]

Moreover, although an experiential deprivation that has already occurred cannot, as a fact of history, now be eliminated (and is in this respect unlike a past structural injury conceivably capable of present repair), the behavioral deficits it might normally be expected to signal may, in certain cases, be erased through modification of *auxiliary* conditions, as we have pointed out earlier. The question of deficit reversal, or of the organism's plasticity – taken in the abstract – is therefore indeterminate until additional specifications are laid down as to how it is to be interpreted. Are we, that is, to take only spontaneous amelioration of deficit under normal conditions as evidence of reversibility (or plasticity) or are we, in addition, to reckon also improvement that results from altering such conditions?

Early evidence for critical periods in the development of social and maternal behavior in rhesus monkeys[7] and imprinting in geese[8] showed that failure of the proper stimulation resulted in what were thought to be *irreversible* abnormalities in behavior persisting into adult life. Similarly, children raised in orphanages were deemed to have suffered *permanent* intellectual damage as a result of early deprivation.[9] Suomi *et al*. found, however, that with the proper 'social therapy,' isolated rhesus monkeys can develop a normal repertoire of social behavior, thus apparently showing the *reversibility* of effects of early deprivation.[10] And Clarke and Clarke showed several examples of severely deprived children who, at the ages of six or seven, developed normal linguistic and cognitive abilities, within an attentive, warm adoptive family setting.[11] Evidence of this sort led certain investigators to minimize the decisiveness of early experience in development.[12] Kagan summarized the debate on this point by contrasting the view that denies the 'resiliency' or 'malleability' or 'modifiability of psychological structures established early in life,' with the view that affirms these properties, holding that the effects of early experience 'are reversible under proper environmental conditions.'[13]

But this contrast of reversibility and irreversibility is, as we have suggested, too stark. It overlooks the distinction, noted above, between two ways of enhancing potential through negation of impediments: i.e. through *eliminating* them or, rather, through *circumventing* them. For in every case cited here in opposition to the alleged early evidence for 'irreversibility,' alteration of auxiliary conditions is involved. The 'reversibility' thereby ostensibly supported might thus naturally be interpreted as a case of *circumventing* rather than *eliminating* the deficit in question, whereas the thesis of irreversibility might be read as denying, not such circumvention, but rather elimination, under normal conditions. The issue has simply not been joined.

Thus Suomi *et al.* require the proper *social therapy*, Clarke and Clarke require an *attentive warm adoptive family setting*, and Kagan speaks of reversibility under *proper environmental conditions*. Both the irreversibility and the reversibility in question are thus, from a logical point of view, *compatible*, considered abstractly. It is pointless to decide between them as if they were mutually exclusive alternatives. The question is not whether organisms are or are not malleable (or modifiable, or plastic), but rather under what conditions certain of their properties may constitute impediments to the attainment of given functions. With the question thus conceived, possibilities of avoidance, elimination or circumvention of the impediments in question may be systematically investigated in the interests of an altered potential.

The intimate connectivity of biological and environmental conditions that has here been illustrated suggests one value to be anticipated from cross-cultural study of potential as capacity. Acquainted only with our own society, we may take it for granted that certain desirable outcomes of learning are precluded, blocked by impediments basic to human nature. Because we naturally suppose the level of attention and support given certain forms of learning in our society to be fixed, we generalize local incapacities into universal limitations. Investigation of other societies than our own may bring to light actual achievements of the very sorts we had supposed impossible, thereby stretching our initial notions of potential. Precluded in our own society, such achievements may be supported elsewhere by higher levels of attention and concern, greater concentration of effort, differing institutional arrangements, or stronger ideological and psychological foundations.

Even where comparison of specific achievements is not available or feasible, the study of alternative cultural arrangements may suggest expanded notions of potential. For such arrangements comprise, after all, variations on the auxiliary conditions of *our* society, relative to which our own conceptions of what may impede learning were initially formed. Reconstruing such conditions as variable rather than fixed, we are led by inquiry into particular variants to ask whether they might not indeed negate the specific impediments we had hitherto assumed.

It goes almost without saying that the study of other cultures may, independently of the question of potential, lead us to rethink the goals and purposes of schooling as they are typically conceived within our own society. We may, that is, be led to reappraise the normative direction of our own social arrangements, to ask how we in fact *do* and how we ideally *ought*, through these arrangements, restrict human capacities and traits or allow them to develop. The cross-cultural study of the way a group's beliefs and purposes open or close various of life's possibilities to its members thus naturally impinges on normative questions of *policy* – i.e. what beliefs and purposes we ourselves should adopt in forming our social environment.

C. PROPENSITY AND DEVELOPMENT

The propensity notion of potential predicts that a designated feature will be acquired *if* certain conditions in fact obtain. An attribution of potential, under this interpretation, says more than merely that the acquisition in question is not prevented by some salient impediment. Yet it does not go so far as categorically to predict such acquisition. It predicts the acquisition only conditionally – that is, it asserts its likelihood if, assuming no positive impediments, certain contingencies obtain.

Potential for an outcome that is unwelcome leads us to speak of being 'at risk.' As earlier noted, Gardner has proposed that, in the case of potentials for desirable skills, we speak in parallel fashion of being 'at promise.' His treatment of both expressions fits the propensity notion of potential exactly: in neither case is prediction made categorically, but in each case a likelihood is affirmed conditionally. Gardner makes the additional suggestion that, as in certain cases of risk, so also in important cases of promise, genetic factors be studied as among the critical conditions. Being 'at risk' for a disease, such as hemophilia, predisposes rather than guarantees that the disease will be contracted. Analogously, he suggests, individuals 'at promise' for a certain skilled performance, such as chess, may be thought of as predisposed to acquire the skill under favorable circumstances, though of course they are not certain to acquire it in any case.[14] The connection between genetic predisposition and environmental circumstance in individual development forms the theme of our next illustration.

Topic II Canalization

In our discussion of the previous chapter concerning developmental chains, we contrasted a 'domino theory of prediction' with an 'interactionist' conception. The main point of the contrast is that the interactionist conception alone requires timed additional conditions at intermediate stages to power the transition to subsequent ones. Elaborating such a conception, McConnell upholds 'probabilistic epigenesis' in opposition to 'predetermination' and 'essentialism,' grounding development in 'an interaction of genetic and environmental factors which constructs outcomes.'[15] Such interaction, however, explains only *development from*, but not *development to*, she argues, citing in this connection the work of D. S. Lehrman.[16]

In considering the process of *development from*, i.e. how development proceeds from one step to the next, prediction of the path requires knowledge of both the genome and the environment. However, we need to explain also *development to*, i.e. the fact that organisms typically move toward certain end-states common to the species, by varying paths in a wide range of environments. This persistent directionality must, further, be interpreted without reversion to essentialism or predetermination. The concept often

77

applied in this connection is that of *canalization*, nicely characterized by Waddington as the difficulty of persuading 'the developing
system not to finish up by producing its normal end result.'[17]

The temptation, in accounting for canalization, is to speak of
'genetic blueprints' not merely as a heuristic device for expressing
that the relevant environmental inputs may be counted on in
certain cases, but as a literal affirmation of 'inborn programs
setting out the course of development.'[18] There is, however, no
need to suppose that predetermination is required to account for
canalization. For it may be supposed (as McConnell suggests in
her review of recent work) that evolution in the relevant environmental range has shaped adaptive buffering processes that modu-
late widely fluctuating external conditions, channeling growth in
characteristic directions. Canalization, or 'development to,' is thus
consistent with the interactionist view of developmental chains
presented in the last chapter.

Canalization, the result of evolution, favors certain outcomes
rather than others within the relevant range of environments.
Language in human beings is, for example, highly canalized: deaf
children reared in the absence of sign language will develop their
own systems of gestural communication, systems that capture
important semantic and syntactic properties of oral-aural
communication. This may serve as a striking example of the fact
that there are ways that cognitive abilities and the nervous system
will develop, given half a chance.[19]

Important as such canalized potentials may be, relative to the
normal environmental range, we must avoid taking them as
canonical for education. Here is where the underlying interactionism of our view must be reaffirmed. For certain educational
outcomes that may be valued, a chain of developmental steps may
be envisaged in which the additional conditions are *supplied by
us* rather than counted on to occur naturally within the 'normal'
array of environments. It is true that the 'growth' and 'development' metaphors transferred from biology to education have typically functioned to promote a hands-off attitude, a posture of
restraint by teachers and parents. The message of modern
education has thus largely been that the child's development
requires input from the environment, to be sure, but not control-
ling input by teacher or parent. Antagonistic to the contrary metaphor of education as 'shaping,' the growth ideology has stressed,

rather, natural learning, readiness, child-centeredness, restraint on the part of elders.[20]

However, educational outcomes are of different sorts, and those requiring our active intervention may be no less valuable than the others. Some outcomes indeed may require no deliberate effort or little such effort on the part of elders, and the wise policy is one of restraint. Language here may serve as our example – or walking, or exploration of the environment. Other educational outcomes do require active attention and effort. Here restraint may become abdication of responsibility for ensuring valuable or needed results.

Contrast, for example, language with trigonometry, or with learning to master the discipline of a musical instrument or the art of living harmoniously and considerately with others. William James once described the 'discovering [of] steps of mathematical identity' as 'repulsive' and thought it wrong to present it to students as 'interesting.'[21] Better, he thought, to arouse their combative impulses in an effort to conquer what goes *against* rather than *with* the normal grain. We must, in sum, not suppose that the potential for algebra is any less real or educationally urgent just because it is *not* canalized. 'Potential' and 'development' are concepts compatible not only with passivity or restraint on the part of educators, but also with activity and intervention by them. Which attitude is to be chosen in any given case depends on the values as well as the facts involved.

Topic III International Development

When we turn from the contexts of biology, psychology and education to that of international development in the period since World War II, we confront a more ideological use of the term 'development,' one encapsulating a particular set of values, a set of factual presuppositions, and a large-scale program of social action. 'In retrospect,' writes Francis X. Sutton,[22] 'there was a remarkable agreement among people in both developing and developed countries that they knew what development was all about and that it could be achieved. The fading colonial powers, the United States, and the United Nations all launched into development programs under conceptions of the beneficient effects of

transferring capital and technical knowledge that now look quite naive or primitive – as ruling conceptions of the past usually do.'
Sutton remarks that

> the urge for concrete action and the disposition to maximize the presumed scope and relevance of technical knowledge have been dominant influences in shaping development cooperation. Both the ideology of development and its practice emphasized matters that were controllable by rational effort and hence, presumably, were teachable by example and formal instruction. With the wisdom of hindsight, we are now painfully conscious of the exaggerations of what could be rationally controlled and effectively taught.

The criticism of such exaggerations is now widely available. The notion that economic growth, powered by financial and technical aid from abroad, would lead poor nations to recapitulate the experience of rich nations and culminate in improved living conditions for their populations has proved too sanguine. The idea that economic and technical factors could be largely abstracted from culture and history and employed to bring about desired social change has been subjected to criticism, as has the assumption that national governments rather than villages and local communities were the effective agents of such change.[23] The supposition that educational systems could serve as a lever to bring about rapid 'development' has also been criticized in light of 'concerns about excessive expenditures, unemployed school leavers and considerable disruption of traditional occupations, particularly in rural areas.'[24]

Each one of the vulnerable factual presuppositions here cited can, in fact, be viewed as the basis of a presumptive conditional prediction implicit in the 'development' ideology. *If* financial and technical assistance are supplied by rich to poor countries, economic growth may be predicted; *if* such growth is rationally channeled by the governments concerned, better health, education, and living conditions for the population at large may be further expected to follow. Such conditional predictions resting on presumed lawlike generalizations across nations make plain the applicability of our propensity notion in the present context. Indeed, it may perhaps be suggested that the international development community considered each 'pre-modern' country to be a *potential* 'modern' one, each 'non-industrial' society to be a *potential* 'industrial' one, each nation afflicted with poverty to be *potentially* free of poverty. *If* only certain factors were instituted, *then* etc., until the eventual target is reached in each case. The criticisms outlined above are addressed to the implicit generalizations powering the conditional predictions involved. The propensity notion thus clarifies the logic of debates over international development; it suggests as well the import of research relevant to the issues in such debates.

When we move from the biological sphere into the psychological sphere, we must immediately acknowledge the realm of belief, desire and intention within which our subjects move. Generalizing about individuals with variable beliefs, desires and intentions is a hazardous business even within a given culture with common language, history and customs. When we venture to generalize across nations or cultures, however, the hazards multiply incalculably. The idea that there is a uniform sequence of stages in national 'development' is no more plausible *a priori* than the idea that there are laws of historical development, or laws of the evolution of cultures, or laws of individual biography.[25] We may be able to generalize in these areas, but conceivably only by taking into account the details of belief and intention, and the texture of want and purpose characteristic of our subjects. The extent to which we can indeed significantly generalize on the basis of certain factors is, to be sure, a matter of empirical research. Such research already suggests that the generalizations implicit in the thinking of the international development community have abstracted excessively from the facts and factors of culture.[26]

There is another respect in which our discussion of the propensity notion of potential relates to international development. We have, in the previous chapter, argued against picturing development as a single line emanating from an initial state toward a target we designate; we must rather conceive of any number of such lines radiating in all directions from the starting state to end-states of variable value. We have also noted the importance of value differences as well as differences even in the capacity to conceptualize alternative lines of development. Thus we must guard against the presumption that it is the developer's asessment that is the critical one, that it is *his* state of knowledge, symbolism, and values that determines *the* potential of the subject.

81

This natural presumption may be expressed in the question 'Why can't other countries be more like us?' The very notion that 'developed' nations are to do something *to*, or *for*, the others lends itself to thinking of these others as objects comprising a field of action or problem-solving for the developers: We, the developed, *are*, after all, the future toward which these others are only aspiring; we therefore already embody their *true* values. The values they now proclaim are therefore not to be taken seriously in their own right, belonging as they do to an immature stage on their road to our present.

There is an irony in the very need to struggle against such an attitude, for the ideology of development was, and is, professedly benevolent, to assist economic growth, improve the state of health and the quality of education, erase poverty. Indeed the very quality of benevolence expressed in such purposes tends to hinder the effort to bring them under reflective scrutiny. Thus, for example, even a critical and well-meaning recent review of human development policies categorizes social and cultural factors as 'noneconomic variables,' viewing them in terms of their possible influence on human development programs – that is, considering the values of subjects only as they thwart or facilitate the developer's plans. When such plans are, in effect, taken for granted, the values they embody are not only themselves unquestioned, but they serve also to exclude serious consideration of the values of those whose lives they are to affect. It is here that one sees, by contrast, the import of our emphasis on pluralism and relativity.

D. CAPABILITY AND CHOICE

The capability notion of potential emphasizes the agent's own decision as effective in bringing about a designated learning outcome. A capable performer of a task is, in general, one who can be relied on to perform properly (in permissive environments), *if* he decides to do so. This is another way of saying that he can be predicted to reach the target state, on the assumption that he tries or chooses to reach it. We have here, then, a conditional prediction of a special sort, one in which the agent's own initiative is the critical factor sufficient to warrant expectation of the outcome in question. Now *potential*, under the present interpretation, is capability directed to a particular sort of outcome, i.e. the learning, or acquiring, of a given feature or property. The enhancement of potential is the empowering of learning.

The capability interpretation, as we earlier noted, represents a special case of the propensity notion – the case in which the '*if*' activating the conditional prediction refers to the agent's own choice. Where a *chain* of such capability predictions is involved, the terminal state of each 'if – then' link must be supplemented by a new choice, to make up the 'if' state of the next link. A skilled performance may be analyzed as such a chain, in which timed choices combine with prior achievements in moving the agent forward to ensuing ones. The critical inputs 'at each juncture are not the environmental conditions we discussed earlier, but the ones supplied by the agent's own choices.

Environmental conditions are of course presupposed as permissive throughout and they may be constant over the period of the whole performance. Yet there is here no 'domino' chain, for new choices are required at each juncture, there being no way to go straight from the initial state to the end state automatically. The process cannot be 'triggered' by its initial phase alone; it stalls unless needed choices are supplied at suitable moments. The critical interaction taking place here links the effects of past choices with the impact of the new. When we talk of potential, under this interpretation, we are thus talking, not of development *generally*, but, in particular, of *self*-development.

The shift from the one to the other places the agent's own perspective and initiative at the center of the action, rather than supposing him to be simply registering whatever influences may be playing upon him. The interest is not simply in whatever factors may move the agent toward the target state, but specifically in the agent's choices as effective factors. Such 'internalization' of the development process exemplifies the whole course of education directed toward the acquisition of skill. The point of such education, in every case, is to make the educator unnecessary. Teacher and pupil must part; the teacher cannot accompany the student through life. What the novice may accomplish under specific instruction and with the guidance of experienced elders is eventually to be accomplished without such aids. The effective support of other agents in the environment is in this way internalized in the student, brought within the ambit of his own choices. His education has become a part of *him*.

The enhancement of capability has been widely reckoned as a central aim of education in general, but it is specifically the capability to *learn* that we take as the core of an important concept of potential. A potential businessman or writer or teacher or farmer is (under this interpretation) one capable of learning to be a businessman, writer, teacher or farmer. And this, as we have explained, means that he would indeed (given a permissive environment) learn the relevant occupation and its associated skills if he set himself to do so.

An underlying conception here is that learning processes have associated arts, skills, methods and means that may, to a greater or lesser degree, themselves be learned, thereby bringing such processes within reach of the learner himself. Thus to increase the learner's potential is to put his future learning in his own hands and, to that extent, to empower his self-determination. To the degree that people are what they learn to be, a person with enhanced potential, in the sense under consideration, is one with increased control over his future.

We have noted that education directed toward skill acquisition is, in general, an empowering of the agent's choice. Our normative emphasis on agency is, in this respect, an affirmation of values intrinsic to education itself. We have also suggested that self-knowledge is facilitated by the internalization of standards of performance implicit in agency. In striving to meet the standards of a certain sort of performance, the agent tends to become aware of himself as responsible for the manner of his action, as capable of effecting his purpose if he executes his action properly. When a new option becomes available, his capability expands, and with it a growing sense of what *he* can do and of the proper conditions presupposed by such doing. The sense of confidence engendered by enhanced agency is a potent factor affecting subsequent action in every related sphere of life.

When, moreover, we think not of capability in general terms, but specifically of the capability to *learn* or *acquire* new traits, skills, or features of any sort, we are thinking of the capability to re-form or re-shape oneself, to use one's present choices to alter one's effective dispositions in the future. Such self-determining capability is the form of potential we have been considering here, and it is a corollary of the normative postion we have taken that we respect such capability and its enhancement wherever they may exist or open up as live possibilities. In Kantian terms, such respect is a recognition of human dignity, a treatment of persons as ends-in-themselves and not merely as means to the ends of others.

Contrasting the effort to 'give happiness to others' with the effort to give them 'command of their own powers,' John Dewey writes:[27]

> There is a sense in which to set up social welfare as an end of action only promotes an offensive condescension, a harsh interference, or an oleaginous display of complacent kindliness. It always tends in this direction when it is aimed at giving happiness to others directly, that is, as we can hand a physical thing to another. To foster conditions that widen the horizon of others and give them command of their own powers, so that they can find their own happiness in their own fashion, is the way of 'social action.' Otherwise the prayer of a freeman would be to be left alone, and to be delivered, above all, from 'reformers' and 'kind' people.

Topic IV Basic Skills and Attitudes

We have urged the importance of empirical study of potential as *capability to become*. What biological and cultural pre-conditions underly such potential, and what arts and skills, methods and procedures, attitudes and prior knowledge, may enhance it? How, in short, may *capability to learn* better exploit the *capacity* to do so?

On the biological side, we have already mentioned canalization, illustrating it with the case of deaf children reared in the absence of sign language, who nevertheless develop systems of gestural communication. Apparently, children striving to acquire communication systems will manage to succeed even against great odds. Biological bias provides an initial assist in a certain direction of learning. Here, then, is a form of *capability to become*, favored by the constitution of the nervous system, a potential that is not itself a product of deliberate educational programs or policies but antedates them.

Are there periods of growth in which, similarly, other such capabilities emerge, in ordered fashion? The 'cognitive-developmental' view of the Piagetian school of psychology may perhaps be understood as giving an affirmative answer to this question: prior to a certain time, given sorts of learning may be precluded or virtually precluded; past such time these sorts of learning may 'come naturally' – they may, that is, be acquired easily, in a manner contingent primarily on the requisite effort. Whether the specific claims made by members of this school of thought are empirically warranted is less germane to the present discussion than the fact that such claims may be formulated in terms of the capability notion of potential.

When we turn from biology and psychology to the concerns of curriculum design, questions as to the sequence and generalizability of educational content immediately arise. Will what is deliberately taught today facilitate the capability to learn what will be taught tomorrow? Will it enhance such potential or not? Is there a natural sequence of subjects, topics or lessons such that learning any member of the sequence is likely to empower the student to learn the next? Is there, perhaps, some explicit subject, method, routine or strategy which, once itself acquired, will enhance the effectiveness of future decisions to learn, over a significantly large range of possible topics or areas?

The educational concept of basic skills is relevant here. Without the ability to read, for example, the books in the library are opaque physical objects; the ideas they contain cannot be acquired merely by intention and effort. The story is told of a professor at an American university, lecturing in Russian, who became annoyed that several people in the audience arose to leave shortly after he had begun. 'Why are you leaving?' he asked. 'We do not understand Russian,' they replied. 'You must concentrate!' thundered the professor. Reading, like the more general case of acquiring a language, opens doors to learning, otherwise sealed. With a knowledge of spoken Russian, concentration indeed enables learning of the oral Russian message. With ability to read, one may learn the contents of a library volume by striving to do so, thus expanding access to stored messages beyond the local context.

It is in this respect that language acquisition and reading ability may indeed be regarded as basic; they enhance potential in the sense of capability to learn, over a very large range – indeed an infinite array of possible messages. Analogous remarks may be made about arithmetical algorithms, which enable the solution of infinite numbers of problems at will. And similar comments apply to ability to 'read' the variety of non-linguistic symbol systems functioning in a society, e.g. forms of art which, once penetrated by the learner, may yield an understanding of indefinitely many particular works or performances.[28]

Basic skills have, in some educational discussions, been contrasted with 'creative thinking.' What sort of contrast might be involved? Consider reading again. The reader may learn something new to himself in reading a library book, but he has not therefore processed the message critically nor has he engaged in creative inquiry – inquiry beyond the application of set rules. Wielding an algorithm in arithmetic is not the same as mathematical problem-solving, which admits of no decision procedure, i.e. a routine guaranteed to yield the solution. Is there, then, some as yet undiscovered method of finding new truths not already covered by rules, a strategy of creative inquiry, as distinct from an ability to decode messages already available or apply algorithms guaranteed to succeed?

The search for a general method of acquiring new knowledge is itself not new. In the modern period, we need only recall the two seventeenth-century classics of the rise of modern science, Francis Bacon's *Novum Organum* (1620), which expounded the new experimental method, and René Descartes' *A Discourse on the Method of rightly Conducting the Reason and Seeking Truth in the Sciences* (1637), whose title well expresses its aim. With the hindsight of three hundred years of reflection, criticism and scientific growth, we can now see that Bacon's and Descartes' doctrines were too optimistic. For, as it now seems, neither Bacon's 'inductivism' nor Descartes' 'deductivism' furnishes a general method for discovery of new truth. The concept of a general scientific method, it has been widely argued, must be conceived rather as a canon of criticism and evaluation than as an organon of discovery.[29] Still, if neither algorithm nor discovery method can be supplied, can we not at least provide good advice helpful to the aspiring learner? Thus is the notion of 'heuristics' born – the idea of strategic advice which, while by no means guaranteeing investigative success at will, may be expected to improve the practice of inquiry by and large, over the long run.

To what extent such heuristics are to be conceived as relatively general, hence *basic* in the sense we have been concerned with, and to what extent local, has been a matter of controversy. Is there one pattern of scientific thinking, as Dewey suggested, or none, as Conant supposed, or a small number, as Schwab proposed?[30] How far can we generalize the fruitfulness of intellectual strategies, of 'productive thinking',[31] of advice on 'How to Solve It?'[32] David Perkins offers an evaluation of some of the recent studies of heuristics over the past several years that is critical but moderately hopeful.[33]

On the one hand, he insists, there is no substitute for particular items of 'field-specific knowledge,' the data of history, or mathematics or social science. No general battery of heuristic advice can *replace* detailed information about the field. Yet, the question whether such a battery, *added to detailed knowledge*, can improve investigative performance remains open. The few studies that have been made have, however, yielded mixed results; some studies report gains after heuristic training by comparison with suitable control groups, others report none.

But Schoenfeld's work with mathematics provides some encouragement.[34] His leading idea is that, in addition to detailed background knowledge and heuristic strategies, 'managerial' principles are needed, reminding students when to apply which heuristic strategies. Perkins' discussion of one experiment of Schoenfeld is as follows:[35]

> In one demonstration, Schoenfeld provided nothing but managerial tactics. The particular heuristics were already in place, thanks to the normal curriculum. The mathematics of concern was integration problems in calculus, and the heuristics to be organized were the usual tricks taught in any first-year calculus course. Students learned these tricks of the trade well enough, Schoenfeld knew. But there might be something else they didn't learn: which trick provided the best bet when. So Schoenfeld prepared written guidelines for the students to help them with their final calculus examination. Half the students in the calculus class, not Schoenfeld's own, received these guidelines, and the other half did not. . . . And the actual outcome? Schoenfeld proved

quite right in his conjectures. The students who studied the guidelines outperformed those who reviewed in their usual ways. Moreover, the students returned estimates of the time they spent preparing for the exam, and those with the guidelines in fact used less time than the others did.

This example is of work in a particular field – mathematics – and both the heuristic principles and the managerial tactics were, as Perkins refers to them, 'genre-specific' though, of course, at a higher level of generality than the detailed knowledge involved. Is there a place still for fully general heuristics? The empirical evidence is meager, but Perkins reports his opinion that 'when genre-specific principles are used, general strategies can add to their power. Moreover, we do not always operate in familiar problem domains. In fact, we encounter new kinds of problems constantly not only as we explore novel subject areas but as we go further in a familiar field. General strategies provide an initial approach that will give way to genre-specific understanding as experience accumulates. Finally, remember that the deliberate search for and use of genre-specific strategies can itself be a potent general strategy.'[36]

In any case, the *concept* of heuristics, as a set of learning strategies applicable over a significant range of inquiries, belongs clearly to that of basic skills, enhancing the effectiveness of decisions to learn. Without guaranteeing the capture of new truths at will, heuristics increase potential in the particular sense we have here been discussing. That is, such heuristics increase the agent's capability to learn, strengthening the likelihood of his learning what he indeed sets himself to learn. The importance of empirical investigations of heuristics is thus interpretable by reference to the concept of potential here under consideration.

We shall now conclude our discussion with some remarks on potential and culture. We have been speaking in this section of potential as self-determining capability, and have taken the respect for such capability as a normative guideline. Yet we certainly acknowledge that such respect is not a factual universal. Norms do not describe what *is* but what *should* be, and we do not delude ourselves that our normative position represents a cross-cultural fact of existence. Indeed, we recognize and have attempted to study variations across cultures in the very conception of the self, in the value assigned to personal self-determination, and in the locus of decision-making i.e. whether in the individual or the group. Subtle and important empirical differences emerge from such study in comparing India, Japan, China and the United States, for example.

It is significant that these differences might be formulated as differences in the capability-potentials of average members of the societies in question. However, it is conceivable that the differences under consideration are rather differences in *social constraints* on individual decision, and not differences in capability-potential. For such potential is *conditional*: *if* the person decides to acquire some feature, he will. The existence of the potential is thus unaffected by the fact that society may prevent or discourage the decision itself.

The question to be settled, then, for any actual difference of the sort we have been considering, is whether it is a difference in *capacity* (i.e. social circumstances impeding decision) or in *capability* (effectiveness of decision) or, to some degree, in both. Would a lifting of social constraints against personal decision-making, for example, reveal an unimpaired decisional capability, ready to flower? Or would an effort be required to enhance such capability, as yet unready to take advantage of new capacity? Such questions might well be difficult to answer in any case, and considerably harder in certain cases than in others. It would be unreasonable to expect that they might be answered in some general way, by formula. They serve rather to guide our inquiry into particular instances of cultural variation.

The underlying contrast between capacity and capability relates not only to the description of cultural differences but also to discussions of international development. In this context, the question is whether such development should be conceived as 'structural' or as 'social-psychological,' or both. The authors of a recent paper, for example, emphasize the importance of both, and also offer a sympathetic account of community 'self-help' approaches in international development. In passing, they touch on the import of self-help for what we have here called self-determining capability. Thus they write:[37]

The total amount of resources needed for rapid human development in most countries is so massive that . . . a significant proportion must be mobilized outside the conventional fiscal system; otherwise, rural development is too costly for most national governments to afford. Community self-help approaches are important in this respect because they provide a way to mobilize resources for development. Self-help also has a wider significance, because when villagers work together in groups they gain a sense of power over their lives.

It is this sense of power which is a reflection of potential as capability to become.

We hope to have shown, in this chapter, how the concepts of potential we have introduced apply to selected empirical materials. The discussion of our four illustrative topics was by no means intended to summarize what is known about the problems we have treated. Our purpose has been rather to exemplify the empirical applicability of our conceptual framework at the various levels of our concern, i.e. the biological, the psychological, the cross-cultural and the educational.

The particular topics we have chosen represent also central themes of any significant approach to our problems: the plasticity and directionality of behavior, cultural diversity and development, and basic skills of learning. In interpreting such themes by means of our concepts, and introducing selected normative considerations as well, we hope to have contributed to a more integrated critical approach to issues of potential.

E. CODA: DEMYTHOLOGIZING POTENTIAL

We began our treatment, in Chapter I, with an attack on three myths of potential. These were the myth of *fixed* potentials, the myth of *harmonious* potentials, and the myth of uniformly *valuable* potentials. The framework of concepts we have substituted for the traditional notion was designed to free us of the myths – thus demythologizing potential. The net effect is to replace the myths by three contrary propositions, each applicable to our new concepts. Thus our framework construes potentials not as fixed but as *variable*, not as harmonious but as *conflicting*, not as uniformly valuable but rather as *mixed in value*.

91

The import of such demythologizing is to highlight the inescapability of choice and the responsibility for evaluation. If potentials are not fixed but alterable, we need to reflect how our own efforts might strengthen or weaken, alter or sustain them. If they conflict, we face the need to discriminate among them. If mixed in value, we need to choose which to promote, which to reduce. Coupled with our rejection of essentialism in favor of interactionism and our emphasis on the relativity of potential, the demythologizing process faces us squarely with choices obscured by the traditional notion.

The traditional myths indeed reflect an ancient view of society as fixed, with durable social functions and a limited number of human talents taken for granted. The choices that are now apparent were then not so much obscured as invisible. The contrast between ancient and modern conceptions is brought out clearly in John Dewey's discussion of Plato's and Aristotle's views of education. For Plato,

> a society is stably organized when each individual is doing that for which he has aptitude by nature in such a way as to be useful to others (or to contribute to the whole to which he belongs) . . . it is the business of education to discover these aptitudes and progressively to train them for social use. . . . But . . . [Plato] never got any conception of the indefinite plurality of activities which may characterize an individual and a social group, and consequently limited his view to a limited number of *classes* of capacities and of social arrangements. . . .
>
> While he affirmed with emphasis that the place of the individual in society should not be determined by birth or wealth or any conventional status, but by his own nature as discovered in the process of education, he had no perception of the uniqueness of individuals. For him they fall by nature into classes, and into a very small number of classes at that. Consequently the testing and sifting function of education only shows to which one of three classes an individual belongs. . . .
>
> But progress in knowledge has made us aware of the superficiality of Plato's lumping of individuals and their original powers into a few sharply marked-off classes; it has taught us that original capacities are indefinitely numerous

and variable. It is but the other side of this fact to say that in the degree in which society has become democratic, social organization means utilization of the specific and variable qualities of individuals, not stratification by classes.[38]

For Aristotle, the division of men into classes is a natural one. As Dewey writes of his view:

> Only in a comparatively small number is the function of reason capable of operating as a law of life. In the mass of people, vegetative and animal functions dominate. Their energy of intelligence is so feeble and inconstant that it is constantly overpowered by bodily appetite and passion. Such persons are not truly ends in themselves, for only reason constitutes a final end. Like plants, animals and physical tools, they are means, appliances, for the attaining of ends beyond themselves, although unlike them they have enough intelligence to exercise a certain discretion in the execution of the tasks committed to them. Thus by nature, and not merely by social convention, there are those who are slaves – that is, means for the ends of others.[39]

The need to search out and evaluate what Dewey refers to as the 'specific and variable qualities of individuals' does not even arise in such a picture, nor, even more obviously, does the educational choice present itself as to which of these qualities to cultivate and promote. The view that human talents are both limited in their diversity and inherent in the nature of individuals reflects a society fixed in its design and functions – meant to arrest rather than to open possibilities of change and choice.

'Every authoritarian scheme,' writes Dewey, 'assumes that [the value of an individual's contribution] may be assessed by some *prior* principle, if not of family and birth or race and color or possession of material wealth, then by the position and rank a person occupies in the existing social scheme. The democratic faith in equality is the faith that each individual shall have the chance and opportunity to contribute whatever he is capable of contributing and that the value of his contribution be decided by its place and function in the organized total of similar contributions, not on the basis of prior status of any kind whatever.'[40] Such faith, taken as a familiar starting point for contemporary reflections on education, should facilitate the demythologizing process we have referred to. For it suggests the variability and diversity of human potentialities, their differing value characteristics, and their capacities for conflict.

Yet, even where such faith is clearly affirmed, the traditional mythology still retains a strong hold on contemporary thought and practice in education. The tendency to presuppose fixed potentials in the student and to characterize educational goals in terms of their fullest exercise remains strong. The supposition that such intrinsic potentials generate approved curricular categories is widespread. And the further notion that various groups of students are intrinsically limited in their potential achievements, independent of other measures that might be taken, is still with us. We shall offer three illustrations of these points, the first concerning *instruction*, the second concerning *curriculum*, and the third concerning *achievement*.

In a recent critique of conventional instruction,[41] David Perkins has suggested that such instruction often fails to improve thinking, making and learning because it operates on certain faulty, tacit hypotheses. Among these, he lists the proposition that 'people learn to think, make, and learn mostly through practice that builds on talent.' As corollaries of this hypothesis, Perkins offers the statements 'you can't teach people how to write; you can't teach people how to solve problems.' This hypothesis, he says, 'leads to many problem sets and writing assignments, but little direct attention to the thinking processes behind substantive intellectual tasks.'

The hypothesis, in effect, assumes that people's talents, i.e. their potentials for certain desirable performances, are fixed. Such potentials may be exercised to a greater or lesser degree, and their actual performances may accordingly be improved up to a point, through practice. But the maxima are not alterable, the potentials cannot themselves be changed. There is no point trying to improve the underlying thinking skills of students; such improvement is precluded from the start by the supposed barrier of fixed potential.

This mythical barrier works to the particular detriment of students who do not spontaneously evolve relevant problem solving strategies. And, as Perkins suggests, even those who do might do better yet with explicit instructional attention to such strategies. Here, it seems, a further demythologizing process would be likely to improve our processes of instruction.

Let us turn now to our second example. The notion of maximal fulfillment of the student's potentials has been criticized in Chapter I, as ignoring the value disparities of different potentials and the conflicts among these. We find this variant in an influential recent report: 'Our goal must be to develop the talents of all to their fullest.'[42] Here again there is no acknowledgment that the talents addressed are of mixed value and that developing certain of these will thwart others. The maximization formula 'to their fullest' glosses over the need for evaluation, deliberation and choice.

In practice, however, choices are inevitable and these choices are typically embodied in prevalent or proposed curricular categories. Thus, for example, the report in question goes on to recommend a curriculum comprised of what are described as 'Five New Basics' i.e. English, mathematics, science, social studies and computer science, with a subsidiary reference to foreign language study, arts and vocational education. Clearly such a listing represents a specific and controversial choice among a wide number of possibilities. Why is computer science exalted to the level of English and mathematics? Why is history given no category of its own? Why is the patchwork category of social studies perpetuated? Why are classics, ethics, logic and philosophy omitted? Why are foreign languages and the arts given only subsidiary place?

The point is not that the recommended curriculum cannot be defended but rather that whatever defence is offered must make plain that specific value choices are involved and not simply a maximal development of students' talents, as independently understood. The curriculum, in other words, is not derivable from a neutral assessment of such talents and their maximization. Rather, the curriculum defines and projects a conception of talents to be developed. It is this definition that requires specific argument over the value choices represented. It is not a mere corollary of talents intrinsic to the student and uniquely maximizable. The further demythologizing we have urged would make these matters clear.

We come, finally, to our third example. The issue has to do with stereotyping groups of students on the basis of what Dewey spoke of as their 'prior status' and so diminishing their 'opportunity to contribute whatever [they are] capable of contributing.' This problem concerns not curriculum but achievement relative to a chosen curriculum. Such achievement depends in part on our resource allocations, as we have already pointed out; it depends also on our attitudes and, in particular, on our expectations of the students.

To suppose, for example, that girls cannot achieve as high levels as boys in standard mathematics and science subjects simply because of their gender ignores the effect of negative expectations regarding their achievement. These negative expectations, baseless to begin with, are rationalized and protected from change when an intrinsic deficiency in potential is attributed to girls as a group. The net effect is further to contribute to diminished achievement, thus helping to fulfill a prophecy false from the start.

A recent statement by a Commission of the National Science Board, addressed in particular to the areas of mathematics, science and technology, makes the general point forcefully and offers additional examples. The Commission finds that 'substantial portions of our population still suffer from the consequences of racial, social and economic discrimination, compounded by watered standards, "social promotion", poor guidance and token efforts.'[43] Resource allocations are uneven and often inadequate, diagnoses are faulty, expectations based on false beliefs:

> The opportunity to learn mathematics, science and technology is at present not fairly and evenly provided to all students.
> Students of high potential are too often deprived of the opportunity to utilize their abilities fully. In the past, such inequalities have resulted from a failure to recognize and develop potential talent, from inadequate educational programs in some communities or for certain groups of students, and from the erroneous belief that many students lacked the ability to learn mathematics and science.
>
> Although progress has been made in recent years, unacceptable disparities in achievement, participation and opportunity still exist. For example, black and Hispanic 17-year-olds scored significantly lower than their white counterparts on the national mathematics assessment in 1982. The national norm was 60.2%. White students scored

63.1%, blacks scored 45.0% and Hispanics scored 49.4%. In addition, although the differences are diminishing, there are still fewer females choosing to take advanced mathematics and physical science courses than males. . . .

All of the evidence reviewed by the Commission demonstrates that disparities in test results are not based on the fact that students of different races, students whose parents do not speak English in the home, or students from disadvantaged socioeconomic backgrounds have inherently different potentials. Indeed, the low achievement scores of a significant proportion of such students can be traced directly to both blatant and subtle racial discrimination (including stereotyped racial attitudes), extreme poverty, and, in some cases, unsatisfactory rural or urban conditions.[44]

The Commission recommends that 'discrimination and other disadvantages due to race, gender, ethnic background, language spoken in the home or socioeconomic status and the lingering effects thereof . . . be eradicated completely from the American educational system,' thus eliminating 'barriers to full educational opportunity.'[45] The demythologizing of potential would aid both in clarifying and in promoting such effort to realize the promise of the democratic faith.

IV

THE EDUCATION OF POLICY-MAKERS

A. INTRODUCTION

This chapter outlines the import of preceding analyses for educational policy. What emphases emerge from our framework as significant for the policy-maker's role? How, ideally, ought the policy-maker to be educated? These questions turn us from primarily conceptual and empirical matters to inquiry into their practical meaning.

We have indeed been concerned with practice from the outset, having construed our efforts throughout as pointed toward a *practical theory* of education. Every profession is guided by a practical theory, whether, for example, in the healing of the sick, the construction of human shelters, or – in our case – the rearing and cultivation of the young. Every such theory is not only multidisciplinary, but also linked inevitably to the world of practice within which the problems of the profession arise. Every practical theory comprises also an ethical point of view requiring an understanding of, and respect for, the human beings whose problems it treats.

Accordingly, we have emphasized the centrality of intention and action in our view of human nature, and the importance of understanding the agent's self-definition in our attempts to comprehend his problems. Further, we have tried to link the disciplinary studies and have illustrated the applications of our framework to issues of practice.

Nevertheless, the previous discussions have been devoted primarily to articulating our conception of human nature,

98

explaining our analyses of potential and developing selected applications. The practical concerns implicit in these discussions must now be made explicit, the emphasis on action and on multidisciplinary study applied to the practitioner's role, and the relation of this role to values further considered.

We said earlier that our project might be seen as an attempt to specify how a curriculum for educational decision makers might be conceived. This attempt is of course not to be thought of as a detailed blueprint for a curriculum, but rather as a set of basic guidelines, of central conceptions and attitudes that should ideally permeate a curriculum for makers of policy. Nor is this attempt concerned with formal courses of study to prepare policy-makers. The curriculum metaphor extends more widely to processes of learning that should go on throughout educational policy formulation, execution and evaluation. And the metaphor applies, further, not just to the individual policy-maker but to all those whose attitudes and ideas affect the making of policy. To think of curriculum is useful if it helps us to answer the general question: what basic conceptions ought to inform the policy process?

B. BEYOND TECHNIQUE

There are important aspects of policy-making and evaluation that are technical in a relatively straightforward sense: they involve special knowledge or methods of analysis developed within a discipline or professional tradition. Questions relating, for example, to nutrition, to neurological disability, to statistical analysis, to agricultural procedures may all be considered technical in this sense. The layman concerned with such questions is well advised to consider the results of the relevant special disciplines, or the consensus of their practitioners on these matters; he cannot pronounce on them himself with any degree of confidence. If the layman is, moreover, to aspire to a policy-making role, he must acquire at least a modicum of the relevant technical knowledge and a certain proficiency in forms of technical analysis and technical evaluation. But the policy-making role cannot be reduced wholly to technical matters.

First, in order for technical items, such as mathematical formulae, theoretical constructs and special notations to be properly understood and applied, their logical bases and methodological backgrounds have to be comprehended: what functions do such items serve in the larger context of inquiry, what are their conceptual structures and their empirical credentials, what alternatives, if any, are available within their respective disciplines, what limits on their interpretation are presupposed? Intelligent use of the results of a specialized inquiry requires a grasp of its underlying logic.

Second, each item of special knowledge must, in policy applications, be brought into contact with items drawn from other special studies. The integration of practical considerations stemming from different disciplines of research typically falls outside each discipline. The architect, for example, must thus deal with and relate the economic, physical and sociological bearings of his design. Such integration is not given within any single discipline; it is not itself a further disciplinary specialty, but rather a matter of professional art. It requires, first of all, a sensitivity to the languages and procedures of diverse special inquiries and an ability to link them, where possible, through translation, or partial translation. Beyond the reach of translation altogether, it requires that one accommodate the various items to one another in assigning them relevantly to different segments of the common problems.[1]

Reference to such common problems provides yet a third respect in which the policy role shows itself to be irreducible to the merely technical. For such problems arise not in a segregated domain ordered for the purposes of inquiry by a given discipline but rather in the fullness of everyday life, the scene of multiple human activities, experiences, purposes and needs. The awareness of such problems is not the monopoly of any special discipline, nor is it the exclusive province of any set of disciplines. Pooling the specialized perspectives of the several forms of inquiry does not yet guarantee human understanding. Such understanding, since it is addressed to the activities and feelings of people, requires access to the way those people understand themselves; it requires that we hear what they say when they speak in their own voice.[2]

The policy role, finally, requires self-consciousness respecting values. This is, of course, not meant to deny that the special disciplines are themselves guided by values; nor is it intended to resuscitate a general dichotomy of facts and values. The point is rather that the values of inquiry are in themselves insufficient to orient the response of professions to the diverse realms of practical life. To heal the sick is more than just to inquire into the healing of the sick, and it demands organization by its own appropriate principles of action.

I have listed four respects in which the policy role goes beyond the domain of technical knowledge and enters upon the humanistic realm. To gather these four aspects together and make them explicit as guidelines for the education of policy-makers is to conceive of the policy role in a distinctive way. This distinctiveness is best understood by seeing what it excludes. It excludes, first of all, the notion that results of special inquiries are hard and fast truths, to be accepted without question and applied directly to problems in whatever ways may seem plausible. The present conception, by contrast, insists that the scope and meaning of every result is qualified by its logical and methodological context. The policy-maker certainly need not, and cannot, become a specialist himself in every discipline relevant to his work. But he can and should be able to raise critical questions addressed to the specialists, concerning their basic concepts and the basic logic of their argumentation.

Second, this conception excludes the notion that policy is the appendage of any single discipline. No discipline enjoys a unique purchase on the problems to be addressed. The education of a policy-maker can therefore not be construed as a process merely of absorbing the abstractions of a single discipline, learning to speak its language and to map its hypotheses onto practice. The policy-maker needs to be multi-lingual, to learn to speak and hear various disciplinary dialects and to employ them conjointly in understanding his problems.

Third, this conception excludes the notion that the disciplines, taken singly or together, constitute the full conceptual equipment for policy roles. The policy-maker, under this conception, should be multi-lingual not only with respect to the several disciplines of inquiry, but also with respect to the ordinary languages of those people whose problems such inquiry addresses. For the very relevance of disciplinary findings is intrinsically qualified by the meanings such people may place on them.

Finally, this conception excludes the idea that the policy-maker is above or beyond the reach of value considerations, that his role

101

is merely to pursue with maximal efficiency goals independently determined.[3] This conception, on the contrary, emphasizes the fusion of technical and value components of action; efficiency in intentional activity is a virtue if, and only if, the intention is proper. The agent of policy inescapably confronts both the question of value and the question of efficiency, if he is at all reflective. He stands not outside the realm of value but squarely within it.

C. POLICY AND PEOPLE

The human studies are reflexive in nature. The student of human nature is learning about himself as well as about others. His very efforts to give a systematic account of human activity are comprehended by the account he gives. A creature of intention and action, he pursues his special goal of understanding intention and action by studying the self-conceptions of creatures like himself.

Understanding his own action in terms of his purposes and beliefs, his norms and the ideals he sets for himself, he seeks a parallel understanding of others. That is to say, he strives to place the action of others within the framework comprised of their purposes and beliefs, their norms and the ideals they set for themselves. The application of such a teleological explanation schema is, as earlier emphasized, of continuing importance in history, social science, psychology, literature and everyday life.[4]

People taken as *objects of study* by social scientist and policy-maker alike are not for that reason to be thought of as *objects*. In so far as the belief-purpose schema is thought relevant to understanding their actions, they are accorded a fundamental distinction from mere objects – things which may be symbolized but do not themselves symbolize, things which may be used to further various ends but which themselves form no ends.

The policy-maker concerned to understand people, as indeed he must, needs thus to view them as subjects – active beings whose field of endeavor is structured by their own symbolic systems, their conceptions of world, self and community, their memories of the past, perceptions of the present and hopes for the future. Treating people as carbon copies of oneself, without taking the trouble to enter into their cultural environment, or – worse still

– treating them as mere instrumentalities for, or hindrances to, the realization of a preconceived plan is a formula for policy failure.

There is a second respect in which people are to be viewed as subjects. They are to be seen not simply as comprising a field of application for policy, but as a resource for its origination and evaluation. This attitude takes their reactions not merely as promising facilitation or defeat of policy but as offering occasions for the review of policy. The policy-maker's advance rationale is not sealed off from scrutiny *by* those, and communicaton *with* those for whom his policy is intended. His initial intentions are vulnerable to change, in principle, through interaction with the intentions of others.

Taking people as subjects means, then, *acknowledging* the existence of their perspectives and perceptions, and it means also *respecting* such perspectives in the formulation of one's own policies, giving no privileged role to one's own perspectives simply because they are one's own. This general attitude we spelled out earlier, in describing the normative presuppositions of the present work.

The combination of acknowledgment of, and respect for, the equal powers of others to legislate rules for themselves is, as Kant taught, a recognition of human dignity. Such recognition means that human development cannot be construed as a shaping, by one agent, of another's life. The other's life is not a piece of clay to be shaped by the developer or the developer's policy. It has its own integrity, its own structure and movement. Any policy for development must take such reciprocity into account, must therefore not pretend that its own goals are beyond question, its own vision of welfare decisive.

Recognition of human dignity as an ideal of policy is a matter of prizing people's powers to order their own lives; it is equally a matter of prizing social arrangements that honor such powers. Policy inescapably influences lives, but such influence is properly directed toward the enhancement of human dignity, thus interpreted. The aim of development is self-development; equally it is social development of a special sort – the growth of arrangements under which free human beings may regard one another with mutual respect for their shared intelligence and powers of choice.

103

D. POLICY AND REFLEXIVITY

I have emphasized the reflexivity of the human studies, urging that in such studies the inquirer belongs implicitly to the subject matter itself. The effect of this point, made explicit, is to turn attention inward, to focus the policy-maker's awareness on the contribution he himself makes to the phenomena he addresses. The movement encouraged is the movement from a naively realist attitude to a self-conscious or critical attitude. Such an attitude is of major importance for the policy role as here conceived.

This attitude is, however, not a natural one; it requires special cultivation. Indeed, the heavy onus of policy responsibility in education militates strongly against it. Self-consciousness increases the burden of choice and enlarges the perception of uncertainty. The pervasive drive to simplify, to objectify, to reduce is thus fully understandable. Educational potentials, for example, have accordingly been petrified into fixed attributes of the child's nature, uniformly positive in value and, as a set, harmoniously realizable. Multiple problems of choice have been reduced to the problem of realizing most efficiently those potentials now manifest. The policy-maker's attention has been focused outwards, on the child and on technique.

The present treatment points in the opposite direction, toward the policy-maker's assumptions of fact and affirmations of value, encouraging a growth of self-awareness relevant to the policy-maker's role. I review here the major components of such self-awareness.

1. Value

If a child has not one but indefinitely many potentials of variable worth, if metaphysical essence does not provide an objective pre-selection among these, and if the total set always harbors internal conflict, the need for some independent selection becomes inescapable for the policy-maker. He must, in short, choose which to attempt to realize, which to minimize, counter or ignore.

Of course, individuals working on policy matters typically work within an institutional framework. Policy does not issue from each person separately but usually represents the institution as a corporate product. In this respect, when speaking of 'the policy-maker,' I have in mind whatever agency is responsible for the policy product, whether individual or – as is the case more typically – institutional. The institution, as well as the individual, needs to become aware of its values, that is, its bases for selection of potentials to realize, by contrast with those it chooses to ignore or counteract. There is an institutional, as there is an individual, responsibility to make value criteria plain and to offer some rationale for them.

However, in emphasizing the powers of choice of individual agents, I have implicitly denied that such agents can altogether be relieved of responsibility for what they do, even when they work within an institution. The implication is that individuals ought to be reflective about the values of the policy-making institutions to which they contribute, by their work or otherwise. They need to ensure that the contributions they make to the policy-making process command their own reflective assent.

2. Culture

A second component of self-awareness is *cultural context*. Here the point I emphasize relates not to the realization of potentials but to their very attribution, for, in such attribution, the assumed cultural context serves typically as a tacit parameter. Change the parameter and you may well change the very attribution; what one culture opens as a possibility for learning may be closed by another. This is an aspect of what was referred to earlier as the relativity of potential. Appreciation of such relativity should serve to draw the policy-maker's attention to his presuppositions as to cultural context.

That this point is of great importance in education may be seen by examining the role of denials of potential. Such denials function to absolve the policy-maker from accomplishing what is alleged to be impossible. If a child does *not have* the potential to become a skilled worker, or a professional, or a musician, or a writer, society surely cannot be charged with the obligation to realize such potential.

When the matter is left in this state, the issue is made to hinge simply on some feature of the child itself; the child is stigmatized as having a deficiency that stands in the way of a desirable outcome. The policy-maker is therefore free to turn his efforts elsewhere – to children *with*, rather than *without* potential. Once, however, the allegedly critical feature of the child is understood to impede the outcome only *relatively* to presumed auxiliary conditions, e.g. certain stereotypes as to race, sex or socio-economic class, the whole policy picture undergoes change. The prevention is no longer assigned to the child alone but rather to the combination of child-and-context; 'interactionism' replaces 'essentialism.'

Cross-cultural studies serve to alert us to the need to relativize our judgments of potential to conditions prevailing in our own culture. Finding, for example, that certain achievements we had deemed generally precluded are in fact realized in some other society, we may withdraw or qualify our earlier generalization of incapaciy. For reasons of this sort, if for no other, it is important that policy be informed by cross-cultural awareness, that policy-makers be encouraged to look at problems not just in the context of their own societies, but in the context of others remote in time, space and character. Historical, anthropological and comparative studies, in particular, ought to enter into the training of those involved in the formulation of principles governing educational efforts.

It may seem paradoxical that in advocating a greater measure of *self*-awareness on the part of policy-makers, I am here counseling a greater attention to *other* cultures. Yet there is here no paradox at all. Self-knowledge is a typical fruit of contrast with others, against which one's own distinctiveness is more sharply etched; this principle applies to groups as well as individuals. Historical and cross-cultural studies, which focus our attention on the customs, achievements and values of other cultures may thus bring about a new perception of our own distinctive values and assumptions.

3. Habit

I have discussed relativity to cultural context in a general way. Appreciation of such relativity, I have argued, alters the picture fundamentally, sensitizing us to possibilities otherwise excluded.

106

But mere possibility, it may be countered, is not enough. The child is after all to be dealt with in its actual cultural context, not in some imagined alternative one. If the actual context is impervious to change by deliberate effort, it does not matter, from a practical point of view, that in hypothetically differing conditions the child's achievement might be quite different.

Here is where a third component of self-awareness becomes important, namely an appreciation of the force of *habits and policies already established*. Policy issues arise always in the context of habits and policies already formed and functioning, or else in the process of being crystallized. The customs, habits, expectations, rules, operative programs and presumptions that form the background of any question of policy are themselves principles of action of one sort or another. They are themselves of a piece with policy and, to varying degrees, often alterable by policy. They are, however, so much a part of the familiar environment that they are frequently not attended to as possible levers of change. But it is often the case that among the auxiliary conditions of a given impediment to achievement lie established modes of action accessible to deliberate alteration. Such alteration may, moreover, yield an alternative context for the child, overcoming the relevant hindrance.

That a child's disability blocks the achievement of a specific sort of learning, for example, may be true only if the available therapy or ameliorative technology is restricted in certain ways. That it is thus restricted may itself be the result of a policy or, at any rate, alterable by policy. Discriminatory treatment of poor or minority children, hampering their learning, is not to be assumed an unalterable fact, inaccessible to policy initiatives. That the sort or level of schooling made available in a given region is inadequate for attaining certain learning outcomes may be a fact that is open to change by policy. Learning outcomes are affected critically by the allocation and distribution of resources established by prior policy. Throwing such policy itself into question rather than assuming it to be a fixed part of the cultural fabric may open the way to the educational outcomes in question.

4. Knowledge

A fourth component of the self-awareness we advocate for the policy-maker is that concerned with the state of knowledge. New knowledge may open the possibility of turning today's incapacity into tomorrow's capacity, thus enhancing potential, or it may open the prospect of doing just the reverse, and shrinking it.

We typically focus just on the enhancement of potential, but shrinkage is illustrated by the development of immunization procedures against certain diseases, thus destroying the undesirable potential of contracting these diseases. The will to destroy such potential was, in itself, obviously insufficient to do so prior to availability of the procedures. Without the procedures, it was more properly describable as a wish, or a hope, rather than a will; it reflected no policy option. The development of a vaccine against polio made possible for the first time an option of policy; it tested the social will to eliminate the disease.

Similarly, expansion of potential may follow upon new knowledge as to how to eliminate formerly preventive circumstances, or else how to alter the context so as to remove their preventive sting. A child afflicted with a physical disability may, for instance, be cured of it; alternatively, auxiliary devices may be supplied so that the disability no longer disables in the relevant respect. The supply of such devices is not an option prior to the development of the requisite knowledge; with such knowledge, it poses a new question for policy, putting the values as well as the will of society to the test.

A variety of distinctions relative to new knowledge needs to be borne in mind. Development of a new fundamental theory may be very far from pointing out some desirable action available to us. It might not expand the effective range of our policy options, no matter how significant it might otherwise be. Even if the fundamental theory is applied so as to furnish the design principles for a relevant prosthetic device – say, to overcome a given disability – the production of such a device may still, as a practical matter, be far off. And production or supply, even if technically feasible, may still fall outside accepted or acceptable criteria of cost or desirability, that is to say, customary policies or reflective values. There is, in other words, a long way to be traversed between the creation of a new fundamental theory and the creation of a new available action representing a policy alternative.

Nevertheless, the policy-maker needs to be aware of the continuum involved here, connecting theoretical knowledge in the abstract with actions falling within the range of present policy. The dynamic of fundamental research needs to be appreciated – its capacity to impinge on practical options not underestimated. Conversely, it is important to see that problems *for* research are to be selected, at least partly, through identification of the practical problems to be solved.

While the policy-maker ought to understand his field of action as alterable through knowledge, he ought to recognize the autonomy of his role in pointing to problems of practice and aiming to live up to a set of values and ideals. That knowledge changes the field of action should not be taken to mean that the translation of theory through technology into policy is inevitable. It is not the case that whatever *can* be done *should* be done. On the contrary, the policy-maker needs to exercise judgment throughout the continuum, exerting critical leverage on the future even as he executes present policy.

The policy-maker, finally, needs to avoid the supposition that action is constrained by natural circumstances, independently of human knowledge. Human knowledge, itself a part of nature, transforms the rest of nature demonstrably and incalculably. To underestimate this power of ideas is not to be realistic but rather to be out of touch with reality. The point is not that ideas can do anything, nor is it that wishing will make it so, but rather that what is predictable, permissible or preventable is not a function of nature to the exclusion of human knowledge and effort.

The geographical setting of a historical episode certainly exercises an important influence on its course, yet it is not possible to specify this influence independently of the state of current knowledge. What harder physical facts could there be, after all, than mountain ranges and distances? Nevertheless, as Olafson points out,[5]

the geography in question is human geography, that is, those features of the natural setting that block or facilitate human effort in one or another of its major areas. Those features of the natural setting have to be described because they stand in some relationship to human need and effort; and they assume their full significance in a historical account only when they are set in the context of a certain level of technology and technological capabilities. Thus, distances have a quite different meaning for purposes of sixteenth-century history than for twentieth-century history because the 'coefficient of adversity' they present is specifiable only for a stipulated level of technology. All too often this interdependence of natural setting and human activity has been forgotten or left implicit in the geographical sections of history books. . . .

The moral is that the policy-maker needs to look not only outward but inward, taking due account not only of 'external' circumstances but of those circumstances as interacting with available or likely knowledge and technology.

E. POLICY AND TIME

I have advocated a multidisciplinary approach to problems of practice, drawing from both biological and social sciences in discussing potential. I have also expressed the characteristic concerns of philosophy with conceptual and valuational issues. But these disciplinary perspectives alone do not suffice for a proper account of policy. They need to be supplemented by an appreciation of historical aspects – by a sense of the temporal dimension of policy. I now address five questions relating to this dimension, turning first to the question of continuity.

1. Potentials and Continuity

Potentials, I have argued, are not fixed, but subject to change as a result of biological or cultural changes, or both. I have, moreover, explicitly built time into the notion of potential, speaking, strictly, of potential *at a given time*. But this is far from providing a sense of continuity linking the present with the past. Nor does it suggest, let alone encourage, the obverse sense of a continuous movement into the future. In solving a mechanical problem, the engineer likewise takes account of the momentary configuration of bodies

110

and the momentary disposition of variable physical forces, but that hardly turns engineering into history.

Policy-makers, similarly, acknowledge temporal variation in the factors that concern them, but they typically maintain an engineering, rather than a historical attitude toward their subject matter. The focus of policy being, in any case, on what is to be done now with the resources available, the emphasis is on the foreground, not the background, the attitude practical rather than reminiscent or speculative. The policy-maker may be keenly sensitive to novel opportunity and, in this sense, alert to the ripening of time, yet fundamentally ahistorical in his general consciousness.

Nor does developmentalism of the Piagetian variety supply the historical sense I have in mind. For such developmentalism postulates the ordered emergence of forms of thought in the child, under specified conditions, as a general fact of growth. It provides an abstract schema of change, focusing on certain formal aspects of mental capacity and discerning a uniform pattern in their emergence. But it does not purport to offer an account of the continuity of educational growth bridging 'form' and 'content,' peculiar to certain children but not all, and extending beyond the limited course of stages postulated. It describes no particular path through time but in effect asserts a set of general laws governing the rise of certain mental capacities.

The interpretation of development introduced earlier, in terms of chained conditional predictions, does accommodate elements of a historical attitude. For it is open to connecting any assortment of different laws together in a single chain, putting no limits on their content or their number providing the requisite particular conditions occur at the relevant times, linking the consequent of one law with the antecedent of another. Thus this concept is not limited to 'formal' aspects of growth and does not restrict the number of stages treated. Moreover, it can trace unique paths through time, where the particular sequence of conditions linking the laws is in fact not repeated elsewhere, thus barring recurrence of the identical chain.

In the notion of a particular chain, we have the germ of the wanted concept of continuity, a tracing of the individual path of a child's growth and education, and an idea of alternative paths that might be followed, given appropriate actions and auxiliary conditions. The waxing and waning of potentials over time, their

111

variation with realization, the interplay of realization with motivation and subsequent learning – all these and yet other educational factors may be integrated into a relatively continuous account of growth, both as it has already occurred, and as it may occur in the future.

2. *Selfhood and Temporal Integration*

Why is the possibility of such a continuous account important for the policy-maker? It is important because he is dealing with people, not objects. While objects are spread out in time just as people are, they have no conception of themselves as spread out in time. Their temporal features may be of interest to us but they do not enter into self-conceptions of the objects themselves, partially determining their further histories. On the other hand, people are not only extended in time, but understand themselves as thus extended, forming their self-conceptions through rootedness in a past conserved in memory and directedness toward a future guided by aspiration. The child's conception of its own potentials is not an isolated thing, cut off from such temporal integration. Its growing powers reflect and stimulate a growing sense of self, and the exercise of such powers closely meshes with developing motivation and adult purpose. The organization of the person's life is a continuity sought across time.

The perception of such continuity in the lives touched by educational policy carries inestimable significance for the policy-maker. The child who comes to school for the first time is continuous in self-conception with the earlier child of family, neighborhood and community. Such continuity requires sensitive acknowledgment by schools. It is not only intrinsically proper that teachers strive to appreciate the backgrounds of their pupils – especially those who differ from them in culture, class, race, religion or native tongue. There is an educational point as well. The memories and aspirations of the child, continuous with the memories and aspirations of its family and community, are threads along which educational matter will crystallize, even as these threads themselves undergo change.

Moreover, the school's own program of studies needs to strive for temporal integration. Often the topic of integration in the curriculum is treated as if it concerned only the synchronous bridging of the various subjects, with scant attention given to bridging across time. But the educational life of the child is continuous. It should not be viewed as segmented into the temporal bits sanctioned by local school practice. Nor should the schooling of children be construed as exhausting the temporal limits of education, continuous in fact throughout the whole course of a person's life. To recognize the temporal continuity of education is, in sum, a major desideratum of policy.

3. *Connectivity of Policy Decisions*

Aside from continuity in the lives of those affected by his policies, the policy-maker needs to come to terms with the continuity of his own actions. His decisions have a temporal dimension no less important than that of the persons he influences. He stands within the same stream of time as they, and is subject to the same drive for self-consistency and temporal continuity. Acknowledging these aspects of his role is another, and equally important, way of embodying a historical awareness.

Policy is not a matter of solving one problem and then, having wiped the slate clean, addressing the next. Each solution leaves its traces, to be felt as part of the subsequent problem that must be faced. Such traces may, moreover, be anticipated to a greater or lesser degree, and with varying reliability: if one of several alternative actions is taken now, where will it lead and what decisional alternatives will it open up? And assuming that such and such conditions arise at that time, what may then be expected as a likely outcome, and what decisions might then be available as options, etc.? The action to be taken at this moment is to be taken in the light of chained expectations of this sort.

The basis of such expectations is the record of past experience coupled with a shrewd analysis of present circumstances. Policy decision, like all action as I have earlier described it, involves both memory and imagination, judging some present course to be an optimal pathway to the future, in light of some recalled past. In this respect, policy is a species of time-binding, like all action. However, because it is a public function, its rationale and evidence need to be made as explicit as possible.

113

Judgment underlies policy, and judgment implies discrimination: some assumptions are better than others, some are plausible, some positively discredited. As just suggested, the basis of judgment is some recalled past. It is crucially important, however, to avoid fastening upon isolated past instances as evidence for policy assumptions. In using the past as guide to the present, critical analysis of the available evidence is what is needed.

4. *Policy-making and Policy-testing*

An implication of this critical attitude is that the consequences of a decision already taken require scrutiny as they continue to occur, since they not only set the scene for further action but test the assumptions earlier made. Such test contributes to the improvement of future decision making, by weeding out falsified assumptions still operative in policy thinking. Learning from experience is thus a matter of retaining a memory of the beliefs underlying a past judgment, and utilizing its present outcomes to check these beliefs. If policy-making is to improve through learning from experience, it must not only look forward to the future but also look back to the past. The role of the policy-maker, construed critically, involves not simply the making of decisions for the future but also the checking of past decisions by monitoring their presently discernible outcomes. He thus not only shapes policy but may also contribute to its improvement.

This critical role is exceedingly difficult to realize. It requires a double consciousness, demanding energetic fulfillment of commitments already undertaken while at the same time demanding a skeptical reserve *vis-à-vis* assumptions underlying these very commitments – a deference to accumulating evidence, a willingness to concede, if such evidence so indicates, that these assumptions may after all have been mistaken, and the policies perhaps therefore wrong.

Not only is the mere 'doubling' of consciousness a hardship; the two attitudes seem to be in conflict. Once a policy is undertaken, the energies, reputations and egos of its agents become invested in it to a greater or lesser degree. The possibility that it may be wrong is experienced as a threat to the self. Psychological forces are mobilized to defend the self through vigorous defense

114

of the policy in question. Defensiveness, denial, and wishful thinking tend to take over and thwart critical analysis. Conversely, a cool skeptical reserve, a wait-and-see attitude pending the evidence, a continuing survey of alternatives to present policy – all these tend to blunt commitment and delay action and, in extreme cases, to postpone action indefinitely in favor of further scrutiny of the evidence from the safe vantage of the ivory tower.

This conflict of attitudes poses the most serious threat to the life of policy. For it polarizes the alternatives and presents us with an impossible choice: either execute policy decisions with total and unthinking commitment, or else refrain from action altogether. In either case, the improvement of policy through learning from experience is ruled out completely. For such learning requires both a continuing audit of past experience and a continuous commitment to act upon the future.

Luckily, the conflict of attitudes in question is nothing like a logical contradiction. There is no purely *logical* bar to the combination of resolute action with critical intelligence; nor is there any natural law forbidding all but dogmatists to act and all but passive persons to reason. What is sorely needed, however, is institutional ingenuity applied to the problem of relating decision and criticism – or, more generally put, theory and practice in the realm of policy.

Policy-making and policy execution need to be constantly monitored to insure that continuing criticism and testing feed back into ongoing activity. The education of policy-makers ought, moreover, to inform their professional selves with the twin values of resoluteness under uncertainty, and the redirection of such resoluteness with changing evidence.

What the wise physician does both in providing definite therapy and in critically revising such provision in light of new evidence is what the policy-maker needs to do. He should feel obliged to offer, at each juncture, the guidance best warranted by contemporaneous evidence. In striving to do so, he may take pride both in his active practice and in his welcoming changes in such practice indicated by the evidence. Criticism of his past practice is no longer necessarily a threat, nor does it in any way suggest that practice is to be shunned in the future. But reconceiving the policy role as a critical role is of course not simply a matter of realigning

115

the policy-maker's attitudes. It involves changes as well in the institutional and attitudinal setting within which policy functions.

5. *Policy, Norm and Community*

A further focus of historical awareness is important in considering the policy-maker's role. It concerns not the decision or the decision chain itself, as solution to some problem of practice, but rather the ramifications of decision into norm and precedent. For every decision inevitably reverberates outward, spills beyond the bounds of the problem, no matter how initially conceived. It creates precedents, activates analogies with the past, helps to form, strengthen or modify a general style, a set of norms that newly influence criteria of consistency in action. Choices generalize, with or without the help of words; all decisions are 'decisions of principle.'[6]

Critical problem-solving is thus by no means the only element of importance requiring reference to past experience. Actions, pointed toward particular ends, are at one and the same time systematic in their significance. In striving to accomplish their ends, they simultaneously strengthen or attenuate a received style of striving, legitimate and embody a type of precedent, reinforce or re-create the normative space in which they were conceived.

This normative space is a vehicle of self-identity, both for the individual and the community. It imposes a broad presumptive pattern on our further action, thus promoting the sense of our durable agency. Our actions ought, then, to be examined not only for clues to their effectiveness, but for a sense of the normative space they help to form. We need to ask not just what success our decisions have brought but what precedents they have wrought, not just what we have done to transform the problem but how our deeds have transformed our selves.

This picture applies both to the individual and to the community. But policy, in the normal usage of the term, has to do with the community in particular, expressing, indeed comprising, the action of a community. Those with the authority to make and execute policies carry others with them along a certain historical path, at least presumptively. The maxims under-lying policy typically refer, moreover, to community interests with considerably longer time spans than the individual life, and they invite coordinated efforts across the generations. Think, for example, of the political interests of nations or the doctrinal orientations of religious associations. Policy thus reflects, and reacts upon, the long-range time-binding of historical communities, possessed of common memories and shared dreams for the future. It is within the medium of such communities, partially shaped by policy, that individual efforts are conducted, individual lives planned, individual choices made. It is because this impact of policy is so pervasive that the historical awareness I have urged is of fundamental importance.

F. POLICY, HISTORY AND VALUE

1. *Action and Policy*

The policy-maker does not stand apart from the people affected by his policies; his agency is of a piece with theirs. His own actions are, thus, like those of the others, formed against the backdrop of an assumed culture, and they serve at the same time to reshape it. His role is both qualified by prior values and formative of subsequent values. As a historical agent within the historical process, he both relies upon, and effects changes in the very patterns of his received world.

We have earlier seen the sense in which human beings, generally, are both creatures of, and creators of culture. They do not receive the culture in wholly explicit form; rather, they are born into symbolic systems and arrays of norms that channel, in advance, the possibilities of their action. Nor do they, individually or collectively, redefine their cultures, in the general case, by promulgating new sets of norms outright. Rather, by the effect of their innumerable and continuing decisions on matters great and small, the norms they receive are elaborated and modified, supplemented, reduced or radically altered.

The policy-maker's situation is subject to this description as well, but represents a somewhat special case in three respects. First, in his typical role as incumbent of an institutional position, his decisions carry greater weight than the general run of individual choices. Second, the scope of his decisions is broader,

117

affecting more people than is usually true of individual choices. Third, his decisions tend to be more articulate, subject in greater measure to institutional demands for formulation; the limiting case of policy-making in fact does consist of outright promulgation.

Nevertheless, the general account we have given applies to the case of policy as surely as elsewhere. Though his choices represent more or less articulate influences in the historical process, helping to reshape prior norms, the policy-maker nevertheless stands within a field constituted by such norms, finding his footing there as he alters the very terrain. Conversely, though his symbolic categories and options for choice are historically presented, rather than invented by him, what he decides to do is not therefore predetermined or powerless. Indeed, the responsibility we have ascribed to the policy role reflects the judgment that what he does may make a vast difference, not only with respect to the specific problems he addresses, but with respect to the normative environment of future actions.

2. *Policy and Judgment*

How is he to discharge his responsibility? I have urged him to be aware of his cultural context and his value role. I have advocated his taking a critical attitude toward his value position, pressing him to make this position clear and to attempt some justifying rationale for it. But where is such a rationale to be found? Having destroyed the blandishments of metaphysical essentialism and the seductive appeal of a formula such as the maximal realization of potential, our discussion has now, in addition, stilled the siren song of historical inevitability. The policy-maker is an agent *within* the historical process, not *of* the historical process. He is neither totally shaped by the past nor borne along, willy nilly, to a future wholly made by others. Neither metaphysics, mathematics, nor history will provide him with an automatic device for deciding what his value role is to be.

Of course, we all know there are no automatic answers, no formulas for difficult questions such as these. Judgment of particular circumstances must perforce be left a large scope for exercise. It would surely be mad to provide a rule settling all policy questions in advance, so that answers to them could be

118

computed instead of deliberated. It is for this reason no wonder that we have offered the policy-maker no direct aid in deciding policy questions beyond urging him to be critical about his values and to attempt to work through some reflective rationale for them.

But how is he to be critical unless there are some principles to apply in criticism? How can there be a reflective rationale unless reflection can obtain some purchase, rationality some foothold? How can there be such a thing as *judgment* of the particular case without attainable principles applicable to the particular case? The fact that there are no formulas for settling policy questions in advance does not imply that there are no general principles representing the value dimension of the policy role. And the fact that these principles must themselves be attained, not through applying some automatic device, but through the process of thinking does not suffice to show that they are arbitrary. 'There are no easy answers' is itself too easy an answer, when taken as sanctioning a nihilism in which anything goes. Recognizing the role of judgment in treating the complexity of circumstance must be joined with a thinking through of basic principles upon which judgment may rely.

3. Policy and Philosophical Attitude

It is in reference to such a process of thinking through that the remarks on normative presuppositions in an earlier chapter, and the discussion of people as subjects, in the present chapter, may best be understood. These remarks are intended, not to preempt the role of judgmental discretion in dealing with individual policy matters, but rather to develop a point of view, a philosophical attitude toward such matters, qualifying the exercise of policy judgment.

What fundamental attitude, then, should the policy-maker take in his dealings with other people? If this question does not imply the quest for a formula, it does not follow that its content is therefore trivial. Answering it in one way rather than another may profoundly affect the quality of activities authorized by policy. A policy-maker concerned simply to impose his values and preferences on others, with little patience for what they want or think, will differ drastically from one who construes his task as promoting

119

and legitimating, as far as is possible, the values and preferences of all those with whom he deals.

The normative attitude adopted here may be viewed as motivated, at least in part, by an effort to avoid these two alternatives. For, to begin with, why should a policy-maker's own values and preferences be imposed on others? What differentiates him as a source of values from those with whom he deals? To suppose his values privileged simply because they are his is to offer a consideration that can, with equal persuasiveness, be used by everyone else. 'They're mine!' is a reason that selects no one's cluster of values, because it selects everyone's cluster without exception. Once this putative reason is generalized, it fails to offer any support whatever to the policy-maker or indeed to anyone else. The policy-maker who in practice continues to exalt his values above those of others, as a general rule and without further reason, is acting simply without a reason, i.e. arbitrarily, giving himself an advantage he does not accord to others. This is another application of the Kantian theme adumbrated in earlier discussions.

Consider now the second alternative we have wanted to avoid – that is, the promoting, as far as is possible, of the values and preferences of those with whom the policy-maker deals. But why should the values of others be privileged any more than those of the policy-maker himself? If 'They're mine!' is no reason for him, it is no better reason for anyone else.

The appeal of this alternative lies in its promise to minimize the need for independent value choice: rubber-stamping the decisions of another requires no further decision of one's own. The promise, however, cannot be fulfilled. For the value decisions of others, taken collectively, harbor conflicts and thus cannot be jointly and successfully promoted. To promote some is to thwart others; promoting any inevitably demands independent value choice if it is not to be wholly arbitrary.

Neither the path of extreme self-assertion nor that of extreme self-abnegation is therefore an appealing route for the policy-maker to follow. But if he is to embark on neither route, he may seem to confront an impossible task. If honoring the values and preferences of all others is no better than honoring the values of none, it hardly seems promising to strive for some optimal proportion that will do the trick.

120

The problem is not mathematical but philosophical: the formulation of a principled normative attitude that will be persuasive and will offer some guidance to the exercise of policy judgment. Such a formulation has been sketched in our earlier discussions in this and previous chapters. Acknowledgment of human dignity, as here understood, requires an avoidance of self-serving interpretations of policy, a rejection of the contempt for others that views them as objects to our own ends or underestimates their capacities to order their affairs. Respect for others does not imply contempt for oneself; self-respect and respect for others are two sides of the same coin, the recognition of human ability to create and re-create general rules by which to live.

4. Policy and Vision

The capability to learn, which we have singled out as a special type of potential, is indeed the power to re-form or re-shape oneself by altering one's general dispositions. Enhancing such potential is, as we have indicated before, an imperative of the position we have taken on normative matters. It is a strengthening of the agent's choice, hence of his freedom in the sense of self-determining capability.

Nor is such imperative a mere rubber-stamping of *de facto* desires. Escape from freedom is indeed, as Fromm has argued, a powerful impulse, to be thwarted not validated. An individual education guided by the aim of empowering choice is not a soft but a hard education, pointed toward acquiring the basic arts, skills and tools of thought. These arts, skills and tools are not automatic growths; they require cultivation and their acquisition is a considerable achievement.

Furthermore, the social arrangements under which the capability for self-development may be taken as a shared goal are far from being merely permissive. They require the hard constraints of mutual respect, of institutions channeling the lawful resolution of conflict, of open criticism and public discussion, of courage to declare one's view and willingness to revise it in pursuit of an intelligent accommodation of interests. The reciprocal acknowledgment of shared rational powers by the members of any community places severe constraints upon its structure and character.

We are, in effect, talking about society as normatively ordered by a democratic ideal, commitment to which has radical and far-reaching consequences, not only for basic political and legal institutions, but also for the educational conceptions that guide the development of the young.[7] All institutions, indeed, operate through the instrumentality of persons; social arrangements are 'mechanisms' only in a misleading metaphorical sense. In so far as education is considered broadly, as embracing all those processes through which a society's persons are developed, it is thus of fundamental import for all the institutions of society, without exception. A society committed to the democratic ideal is one that makes peculiarly difficult and challenging demands of its members; it accordingly also makes stringent demands of those processes through which its members are educated.

As a principle of social organization, the democratic ideal aims so to structure the arrangements of society as to rest them ultimately upon the freely given consent of its members. Such an aim requires the institutionalization of reasoned procedures for the critical and public review of policy. It demands that judgments of policy be viewed not as the fixed privilege of any class or élite but as the common task of all and it requires the supplanting of arbitrary and violent alteration of policy with institutionally channeled change ordered by reasoned persuasion and informed consent.

Now the power to reshape one's dispositions – hence oneself – through choice, implies that one's present dispositions may be viewed as provisional. The capability to learn is the capability to alter what one is and has been; it places the present at risk. Made quite general, such capability is consonant with the vision of a democratic society, in which learning is not restricted but opened wide, in which the risks of learning are more than justified by the human quality of the community sustaining them. The social context for each learner, to be sure, sets the stage for his or her own striving. Presupposed as the condition of individual efforts, such context is nevertheless itself not fixed but provisional, subject as well to alteration through social choice. The peculiar bond that holds such a community together through change and the prospect of change is the mutual respect of learners for one another, and the common stake they recognize in perpetuating such respect.

The demands made upon education in accord with the democratic ideal are stringent indeed. These demands are, however, not ancillary but essential to it. Ralph Barton Perry has well expressed the main points as follows:[8]

> Education is not merely a boon conferred by democracy, but a condition of its survival and of its becoming that which it undertakes to be. Democracy is that form of social organization which most depends on personal character and moral autonomy. The members of a democratic society cannot be the wards of their betters; for there is no class of betters. . . . Democracy demands of every man what in other forms of social organization is demanded only of a segment of society. . . . Democratic education is therefore a peculiarly ambitious education. It does not educate men for prescribed places in life, shaping them to fit the requirements of a preexisting and rigid division of labor. Its idea is that the social system itself, which determines what places there are to fill, shall be created by the men who fill them. It is true that in order to live and to live effectively men must be adapted to their social environment, but only in order that they may in the long run adapt that environment to themselves. Men are not building materials to be fitted to a preestablished order, but are themselves the architects of order. They are not forced into Procrustean beds, but themselves design the beds in which they lie. Such figures of speech symbolize the underlying moral goal of democracy as a society in which the social whole justifies itself to its personal members.

To see how radical such a vision is in human history, we have only to reflect how differently educaton has been conceived. In traditional authoritarian societies, education has typically been thought to be a process of perpetuating the received lore, considered to embody the central doctrines upon which human arrangements were based. These doctrines were to be inculcated through education; they were not to be questioned. Since, however, a division between the rulers and the ruled was fundamental in such societies, the education of governing élites was sharply differentiated from the training and opinion-formation reserved for the masses. Plato's *Republic*, the chief work of educational philosophy in our ancient literature, outlines an education for the rulers in a hierarchical utopia in which the rest of the members are to be deliberately nourished on myths.

In nondemocratic societies, education is two-faced: it is a weapon or an instrument for shaping the minds of the ruled in accord with the favored myth of the rulers; for the rulers, however, it is an induction into the prerogatives and arts of rule, including the arts of manipulating the opinions of the masses.

The democratic ideal precludes the conception of education as an *instrument* of rule; it is antithetical to the idea of rulers shaping or molding the mind of the pupil. The function of education in a democracy is rather to liberate the mind, strengthen its critical powers, inform it with knowledge and the capacity for independent inquiry, engage its human sympathies, and illuminate its moral and practical choices. This function is, further, not to be limited to any given subclass of members, but to be extended, in so far as possible, to all citizens, since all are called upon to take part in processes of debate, criticism, choice, and cooperative effort upon which the common social structure depends. The Kantian notion of a kingdom of ends is of a community in which each member is both sovereign and subject. In Perry's words, 'A democracy which educates for democracy is bound to regard all of its members as heirs who must so far as possible be qualified to enter into their birthright.'[9]

The theme of mutual respect and the emphasis on strengthening the mind's critical powers are closely related. They are linked through the concept of a *claim*, as earlier discussed in connection with value assertions. The language of moral judgment clearly illustrates the point. To say that an action is *right*, or that some course *ought* to be followed is not simply to express one's taste or preference; it is also to make a claim. It is to convey that the judgment is backed by reasons, and it is further to invite discussion of such reasons. It is, finally, to suggest that these reasons will be found compelling when looked at objectively, that is to say, taking all relevant facts and interests into account and judging the matter as fairly as possible. To make a claim is, typically, to rule out the simple expression of feelings, the mere giving of commands, or the mere citation of authorities. It is to commit oneself, at least in principle, to a superordinate point of view, that is, to the

124

judgment that one's recommended course has a rationale which can be seen by anyone taking the trouble to survey the situation comprehensively, with impartial and sympathetic consideration of the interests at stake, and with respect for the persons involved in the issue. To assess the claims of others critically, and to expose one's own claims to the critical scrutiny of others are two sides of the same coin.

Can such mutuality be realized? Does the democratic ideal have any roots in reality or is it a mere fantasy? Difficult as it may be, and far as it is from full historic achievement, the reciprocity of respect implied by this ideal is at least implicit in the pervasive efforts of human beings to explain themselves, to justify their actions, to offer reasons for what they do.[10] They thus in effect appeal to the judgment of others, otherwise situated and differing in their interests and perceptions, to adjudicate the matter impartially. Policy-makers, in particular, do not simply enunciate policy, they propound and support it with reasons, inviting or anticipating counter-arguments to be taken into account or defended against. Even if such activity is sometimes, or even frequently, sham, a policy argument, once publicized, invites responses not wholly controllable. Moreover, the very need to make a show of genuine respect for the intelligence of others indicates the hold such respect has on the imagination of mankind, and allows the hope that it may expand its purchase on reality.

In any case, the function of a normative attitude is not to reflect what already exists but to orient action toward what should be. The vision of human dignity and mutual respect that we have outlined performs this limited but fundamental function. It is not a program but a vision; it gives no operational details but rather a principle which needs filling out and translation into the concrete. It is abstract in a further sense as well, sketching a framework of the moral aspect of action, within which particular paths of life and different pursuits of happiness may all find their place. Like science, it appeals to the common rationality of mankind, contructing a bridge across the historic and cultural chasms that divide human beings. Like the scientific attitude, it too provides no firm formulas, no finalities, no hard guarantees – much that is opaque and controversial remaining at each juncture to challenge our best efforts to apply it. Yet, like the ideal of scientific understanding, which we have also adopted as our guide in these studies, it presents a rational hope, enhancing as well as reflecting the shared human powers of a variegated humanity.

NOTES

INTRODUCTION

1 *The Bernard van Leer Foundation Newsletter*, The Hague, 33 (Spring 1982), p. 12.
2 *The Programme for the Eighties* (copy for information), Bernard van Leer Foundation, Board of Trustees, The Hague (26 April 1982), p. 1.
3 Howard Gardner, *Frames of Mind* (New York: Basic Books, 1983).
4 For the notion of 'practical theory,' see Paul H. Hirst, 'Philosophy and Educational Theory,' *British Journal of Educational Studies*, vol. XII, no. 1 (November 1963), pp. 51–64. On the relation of disciplines to educational practice, see my 'Is Education a Discipline?' in John Walton and James L. Kuethe, eds, *The Discipline of Education* (Madison: University of Wisconsin Press, 1963); reprinted in my *Reason and Teaching* (Indianapolis: Bobbs-Merrill, 1973), pp. 45–57. On the application of various disciplines to problems of practice, see Joseph J. Schwab, *Science, Curriculum, and Liberal Education: Selected Essays*, ed. Ian Westbury and Neil J. Wilkof (University of Chicago Press, 1978), esp. Part III.

CHAPTER I HUMAN NATURE AND VALUE

1 A preliminary account of some ideas in this and the following chapter was given in my 'Human Nature and Potential' (AESA R. Freeman Butts Lecture, 1982), *Educational Studies*, vol. 14, no. 3 (Fall 1983), pp. 211–24. A briefer version of some ideas in Chapter IV appeared in my 'On the Education of Policymakers,' *Harvard Educational Review*, vol. 54, no. 2 (May 1984), pp. 152–65.

2 William James, *The Principles of Psychology* (1890; reprint, New York: Dover, 1950, vol. 1), pp. 121–2. On James' view of habit, see my *Four Pragmatists* (London: Routledge & Kegan Paul, 1974), pp. 122 ff.

3 See John Dewey, *Reconstruction in Philosophy*, enlarged edition (Boston: Beacon Press, 1948, 1957), pp. 57–8 for the contrast between ancient and modern notions of potentiality, with respect to change.

4 For a recent variant, compare B. F. Skinner's statement, 'the goal of education should be nothing short of the fullest possible development of the human organism,' in Skinner 'Why We Need Teaching Machines,' *Harvard Educational Review*, XXXI (1961), p. 398. See also the criticism of this view in my 'A Note on Behaviorism as Educational Theory,' *Harvard Educational Review*, XXXII (1962), pp. 210–13; reprinted in my *Reason and Teaching* (Indianapolis: Bobbs-Merrill, 1973), pp. 165–70.

5 James' choice of careers to illustrate incompatibility may be queried on factual grounds, but his general idea is hardly debatable: consider the career combinations of heavyweight boxer and ballet dancer, automobile mechanic and dressmaker, cardiovascular surgeon and longshoreman, etc. Even for James' example it is true that *from the fact that* a youth has the potential for the one career and the potential for the other, *it does not follow* that he has the potential for both together. Finally, combinations that are not impossible may yet be highly improbable or difficult to realize.

6 On these and related points, see John Passmore, *The Perfectibility of Man* (London: Duckworth, 1970), pp. 18–19 and elsewhere.

7 The account of human nature as active, purposive, symbol-forming, norm-creating, value-directed and emotive, as well as systematic, is influenced by a variety of sources in philosophy, psychology and social science. In its broad outlines, it draws most directly upon the work of pragmatic philosophers, for discussion of which see my *Four Pragmatists*. It is also indebted to Ernst Cassirer's neo-Kantian 'philosophy of symbolic forms,' for which see his *An Essay on Man* (New Haven: Yale University Press, 1944); and Nelson Goodman's *Languages of Art* (Indianapolis: Hackett, 1976).

8 On John Dewey's important discussions of ends and means, his distinction between ends and ends-in-view, and his notion of the continuum of ends-means, see his *Human Nature and Conduct* (New York: Holt, 1922), part three, section IX; his *Theory of Valuation* (University of Chicago Press, 1939), pp. 33–50; and brief passages in his *Logic: The Theory of Inquiry* (New York: Holt, 1938), pp. 167–8, 496–7. See also my *Four Pragmatists*, pp. 227–39.

9 For general discussion of symbolism, see, in addition to the references in note 7 above, George H. Mead, *Mind, Self and Society* (University of Chicago Press, 1934), and discussion of Mead in *Four Pragmatists*, part three. For a systematic analysis of the variety of symbol systems, see Goodman, *Languages of Art*.

10 For discussion of teleological explanation, see my *The Anatomy of*

Inquiry (New York: Knopf, 1963; now Indianapolis: Hackett, 1981), pp. 76–123; and C. G. Hempel, *Aspects of Scientific Explanation* (New York: Free Press, 1975), pp. 254–6, 303–4, 325–9. It is of interest to note that teleology, though 'largely expunged from the natural sciences,' is making a comeback in the field of computer science, though the significance of such comeback is a matter of controversy. For the notion of 'complete rationality' as a model from which deviations may be estimated, see discussion of 'the zero method' in Karl R. Popper, *The Poverty of Historicism* (London: Routledge & Kegan Paul, 1957), p. 141. A recent comprehensive treatment of teleological explanation in the context of philosophy of history is given by Frederick A. Olafson, *The Dialectic of Action* (University of Chicago Press, 1979). (I am inclined to give a greater role than Olafson does to the failures of action and thus to weave teleological explanations into a 'causal' fabric.)

11 For a general discussion of the problems involved in attributing beliefs, see my *Conditions of Knowledge* (University of Chicago Press, 1965, 1983), chapter 4, and Carl G. Hempel, 'Rational Action,' *Proceedings and Addresses of the American Philosophical Association*, XXXV (Yellow Springs, Ohio: Antioch Press, 1962), pp. 5–23.

12 C. S. Peirce remarks that the child's understanding of his own knowledge is often fanciful. 'In many cases, he will tell you that he never learned his mother tongue; he always knew it, or he knew it as soon as he came to have sense.' See Peirce, 'Questions Concerning Certain Faculties Claimed for Man' (1868), in C. Hartshorne and P. Weiss, eds, *Collected Papers of Charles Sanders Peirce* (Cambridge, Mass.: Harvard University Press, 1931–58), vol. 5. 218. Peirce, in the course of this paper, presents a theory of the development of self-consciousness, in which language and testimony play a large role. What I have been concerned with in the text is the *further* development of self-consciousness about one's own *symbolic representations*. (See also *Four Pragmatists*, pp. 44–9.)

13 The notion of a uniquely human 'time-binding capacity,' involving transmission of ideas from generation to generation, may be found in Alfred Korzybski, *The Manhood of Humanity: The Science and Art of Human Engineering* (New York: E. P. Dutton, 1921). The notion of time-binding as integral to human action and intention is expressed in Olafson, *The Dialectic of Action*, p. 51 and elsewhere. My discussion in the text is influenced by his treatment as well as by Dewey's theory of thinking; see *Four Pragmatists*, p. 217, referring to Dewey's *Human Nature and Conduct*.

14 Immanuel Kant, *Foundations of the Metaphysics of Morals* (1785) second section. The English quotation in the text draws upon two translations: that of Lewis White Beck, under the above title (Indianapolis: Bobbs-Merrill, 1959), p. 29, and that of H. J. Paton, under the title *The Moral Law* (London: Hutchinson, 1948, 1972), p. 76.

15 Mead, *Mind, Self and Society*, p. 138. (See also *Four Pragmatists*, pp. 163 ff.)

16 Plato, 'Euthyphro,' 'Apology.' See also A. E. Taylor, *Socrates* (Boston: Beacon), 1952.

17 For the Socratic view, see Plato, 'Protagoras' and Taylor, *Socrates*, pp. 140 ff. For Aristotle's view, see his *Nicomachean Ethics*, book VII. Also see, for a discussion of Aristotle's ethical and educational views, William K. Frankena, *Three Historical Philosophies of Education* (Chicago: Scott Foresman, 1965); on weakness of will see specifically pp. 43–4.

18 See, for example, Kurt Baier, *The Moral Point of View* (Ithaca: Cornell University Press, 1958); William K. Frankena, *Ethics* (Englewood Cliffs, NJ: Prentice-Hall, 1963); R. S. Peters, *Ethics and Education* (London: George Allen & Unwin, 1966).

19 Cp. Dewey, *Art as Experience* (New York: Capricorn Books, G. P. Putnam's Sons, 1934, 1958), p. 131; and his *Logic: The Theory of Inquiry*, pp. 372–4.

20 R. M. Hare, *The Language of Morals* (Oxford: Clarendon Press, 1952).

21 See Paton, *The Moral Law*, pp. 21, 66.

22 See my 'In Praise of the Cognitive Emotions,' *Teachers' College Record*, vol. 79, no. 2 (1977), pp. 171–86, esp. 172–3, and references cited in note 2. This paper is reprinted as Appendix B in my *Science and Subjectivity* 2nd edition (Indianapolis: Hackett, 1982). Note, in particular, John Rawls, *A Theory of Justice* (Cambridge, Mass.: Harvard University Press, 1971), sections 67, 73–5.

23 Kant, in Paton, op. cit., esp. fn.** on p. 66. My version in the text is somewhat stronger than Kant's. Kant speaks of the respect in question not as *involving*, but as *analogous to*, both love and fear.

24 Dewey, *Theory of Valuation*.

25 See *Four Pragmatists*, pp. 197 ff. and Dewey, *The Quest For Certainty* (New York: Minton Balch, 1929). The themes referred to in the text reflect general pragmatic emphases evident e.g. in Peirce's view of meaning and in Mead's emphasis on self-control through anticipation of the consequences of one's acts.

26 See *Four Pragmatists*, p. 219, and references therein to Dewey's *Human Nature and Conduct*.

27 On distinctions of this sort, see e.g. Frankena, op. cit.

28 The discussion to follow concerns Kant's *Foundations of the Metaphysics of Morals*. My reading of Kant's views has been influenced by M. G. Singer, *Generalization in Ethics* (New York: Alfred A. Knopf, 1961), chapters VIII and IX. I have also profited from R. P. Wolff, *The Autonomy of Reason* (New York: Harper & Row, 1973).

29 From the Lewis White Beck translation, *Foundations of the Metaphysics of Morals*, p. 47. (It is important to distinguish the Principle of the Categorical Imperative from particular categorical imperatives.)

30 See Translator's Introduction, in ibid., pp. xix–xx.

31 On this distinction, see Singer, *Generalization in Ethics*, pp. 219–227.

32 Beck, op. cit., p. 36.

33 Paton, op. cit., pp. 96–7.

34 Ibid., p. 95.
35 See my *Science and Subjectivity*, 2nd edition (Indianapolis: Hackett, 1982), pp. 1–2.

CHAPTER II POTENTIAL: A CONCEPTUAL FRAMEWORK

1 Aristotle, *Metaphysics*, book V, ch. 4; book VII, ch. 4, esp. 1029b15; book IX, esp. 105a7–10.
2 Cp. John Dewey, *Reconstruction in Philosophy* (Boston: Beacon Press, 1948, 1957) p. 57: 'Terms which sound modern, words like potentiality and development abound in Aristotelian thought, and have misled some into reading into his thought modern meanings. But the significance of these words in classic and medieval thought is rigidly determined by their context. Development holds merely of the course of changes which takes place within a particular member of the species. It is only a name for the predetermined movement from the acorn to the oak tree. . . . Development, evolution, never means, as in modern science, origin of new forms, a mutation from an old species, but only the monotonous traversing of a previously plotted cycle of change. So potentiality never means, as in modern life, the possibility of novelty, of invention, of radical deviation, but only that principle in virtue of which the acorn becomes the oak.'
3 On explanatory and predictive defects of vitalistic references to entelechies in biology, see Carl G. Hempel, *Aspects of Scientific Explanation* (New York: Free Press, 1965), pp. 257, 304, 433; on vitalism and development, see Ernest Nagel, *The Structure of Science* (New York: Harcourt, Brace & World, 1961), pp. 427 ff. and Nagel, *Teleology Revisited* (New York: Columbia University Press, 1979) pp. 260 ff.

For a general critique of essentialism (with discussion of Aristotle), see Karl R. Popper, *The Open Society and its Enemies* (London: Routledge & Kegan Paul, 3rd edition, 1957), vol. I, pp. 31 ff., vol. II, pp. 5–16. For an interpretation and criticism of Aristotelian essentialism, see W. V. Quine, *From a Logical Point of View* (Cambridge, Mass.: Harvard University Press, 2nd edition, 1961), pp. 22, 155 ff.

On teleological explanation generally, see my *The Anatomy of Inquiry* (Indianapolis: Hackett, 1981), pp. 76–123. For a more favorable view of Aristotle's teleological notions, see Martha C. Nussbaum, *Aristotle's De Motu Animalium* (Princeton University Press, 1978), Essay I, pp. 59–106.
4 Aristotle, *Metaphysics*, book IX, 1049b–1051a.
5 John Passmore, *The Perfectibility of Man* (London: Duckworth, 1970), p. 19, italics in original. See also his references to Augustine, Aquinas, Descartes, Spinoza and Leibniz in connection with this tradition, pp. 18–19.

6 See Gilbert Ryle, *The Concept of Mind* (London: Hutchinson, 1949), pp. 126 ff., esp. pp. 127, 131. My treatment of capacity and preventive circumstances here draws upon chapter 5 of my *Conditions of Knowledge* (University of Chicago Press, 1983), pp. 91 ff.

7 Cp. Ryle, *The Concept of Mind*, pp. 132–3, and the references to propensities in *Conditions of Knowledge*.

8 This idea has been proposed as an account of genetic explanation by Ernest Nagel, *The Structure of Science* (New York: Harcourt, Brace & World, 1961), pp. 564–68, and by Carl G. Hempel, *Aspects of Scientific Explanation* (New York: Free Press, 1965), pp. 447–53.

9 The engine example is that of William Dray, *Laws and Explanation in History* (Oxford University Press, 1957), pp. 66–72. The point that the set of sub-laws implies, hence accounts for, the global law connecting oil leak to engine failure is made by Hempel, *Aspects of Scientific Explanation*, p. 452.

10 G. E. Moore, *Ethics* (New York: Oxford University Press, 1949), pp. 127–8.

11 For discussion of a related point, see my treatment of 'the timid student' in *Conditions of Knowledge*, pp. 65–6.

CHAPTER III THE FRAMEWORK APPLIED AND ILLUSTRATED

1 W. D. Wall, 'Research and the Bernard van Leer Foundation,' *International Journal of Behavioral Development*, 1 (1978), pp. 265–87, esp. pp. 271, 285.

2 See G. K. Von Noorden, 'Classification of Amblyopia,' *Amer. J. Ophthal.*, 63 (1967), pp. 238–44.

3 See P. B. Dews and T. N. Wiesel, 'Consequences of Monocular Deprivation on Visual Behavior in Kittens,' *J. Physiol. (Lond.)*, 206 (1970), pp. 437–55.

4 See D. H. Hubel and T. N. Wiesel, 'The Period of Susceptibility to the Physiological Effects of Unilateral Eye Closure in Kittens,' *J. Physiol. (Lond.)*, 206 (1970), pp. 419–36.

5 Susan McConnell, 'The Effects of Early Experience on the Brain: Implications for the Study of Human Potential,' unpublished paper, Harvard Project on Human Potential, no. IIa (1981), p. 55.

6 Howard Gardner, *Frames of Mind* (New York: Basic Books, 1983), p. 38.

7 H. F. Harlow and M. K. Harlow, 'Learning to Love,' *American Scientist*, 54 (1966), pp. 244–72.

8 K. Lorenz, 'Companions as Factors in the Bird's Environment,' in K. Lorenz, ed., *Studies on Animal and Human Behavior* (Cambridge, Mass.: Harvard University Press, 1970).

9 H. C. Haywood, 'Experiential Factors in Intellectual Development: The Concept of Dynamic Intelligence,' in J. Zubin and G. Jervis,

eds, *Psychopathology of Mental Development* (New York: Grune & Stratton, 1967): and H. M. Skeels, 'Adult Status of Children with Contrasting Early Life Experiences,' *Monogr. Soc. Res. Child Develop.*, 31 (1966), pp. 1–65.

10 S. J. Suomi, R. Delizio and H. F. Harlow, 'Social Rehabilitation of Separation-induced Depressive Disorders in Monkeys,' *Am. J. Psychiat.*, 133 (1976), pp. 1279–85.

11 A. M. Clarke and A. D. B. Clarke, *Early Experience: Myth and Evidence* (New York: Free Press, 1976).

12 J. Kagan and R. E. Klein, 'Cross-cultural Perspectives on Early Development,' *American Psychologist*, 28 (1973), pp. 947–61.

13 J. Kagan, 'Resilience and Continuity in Psychological Development,' in A. M. Clarke and A. D. B. Clarke, eds, *Early Experience: Myth and Evidence*.

14 Gardner, *Frames of Mind*, p. 35.

15 Susan McConnell, 'Two Biological Perspectives on Species-Typical Development,' unpublished paper, Harvard Project on Human Potential (1981), p. 31. On probabilistic epigenesis, see G. Gottlieb, 'Conceptions of Prenatal Behavior,' in L. R. Aronson, E. Tobach, D. S. Lehrman and J. S. Rosenblatt, eds, *Development and Evolution of Behavior* (San Francisco: W. H. Freeman, 1970).

16 D. S. Lehrman, 'Semantic and Conceptual Issues in the Nature-Nurture Problem,' in ibid.

17 C. H. Waddington, *The Evolution of an Evolutionist* (Ithaca: Cornell University Press, 1975), quoted in Gardner, *Frames of Mind*, p. 38. On canalization, see Gardner's discussion in ibid., pp. 36 ff.

18 See discussion in R. F. Kitchener, 'Epigenesis: The Role of Biological Models in Developmental Psychology,' *Hum. Dev.*, 21 (1978), pp. 141–60.

19 These points have been emphasized by Howard Gardner. See his *Frames of Mind*, pp. 52, 86.

20 See my *The Language of Education* (Springfield: Charles C. Thomas, 1960), ch. III, 'Educational Metaphors,' esp. pp. 49 ff.

21 William James, *Talks to Teachers* (New York: Norton, 1958 [originally published by Henry Holt, 1901], chs 7 and 11, pp. 51, 83.

22 Francis X. Sutton, 'Rationality, Development and Scholarship,' *Items*, Social Science Research Council, vol. 36, no. 4 (1982), pp. 49–58. The quotations to follow are taken from pp. 50 and 51.

23 See Paul Streeten, *First Things First* (Oxford University Press for the World Bank, 1981). For a brief review, see Streeten, 'From Growth to Basic Needs,' *Poverty and Basic Needs* (Washington, DC: World Bank, September 1980), pp. 5–8. See also *World Development Report* (Washington DC: World Bank, 1980), and Everett M. Rogers, Nat J. Colletta and Joseph Mbindyo, 'Social and Cultural Influences on Human Development Policies and Programs' (reprinted from 'Implementing Programs of Human Development') *World Bank Staff Working Paper*, no. 403 (Washington, DC: World Bank, July 1980).

24 Sutton, op. cit., p. 54 and see Ronald Dore, *The Diploma Disease* (Berkeley: University of California Press, 1976).
25 See, e.g., Morris R. Cohen and Ernest Nagel, *An Introduction to Logic and Scientific Method* (New York: Harcourt Brace, 1934), pp. 344–7; and Karl R. Popper, *The Poverty of Historicism* (London: Routledge & Kegan Paul, 1957).
26 This point has been emphasized by my project colleagues Robert LeVine and Merry White, and will be treated in their co-authored project volume, *Human Conditions: The Cultural Factor in Educational Development* (to appear), esp. ch. 1.
27 John Dewey, *Human Nature and Conduct* (New York: Holt, 1922), part four, section I, 'The Good of Activity.'
28 For general analysis and discussion, see Nelson Goodman, *Languages of Art* (Indianapolis: Hackett, 1976).
29 For critique of Bacon and Mill, cp. Cohen and Nagel, op. cit., pp. 245 ff.
30 See J. A. Easley, Jr, 'Is the Teaching of Scientific Method a Significant Educational Objective?' in Israel Scheffler, ed., *Philosophy and Education* (Boston: Allyn & Bacon, 1958), 1st edition, pp. 154–79. For Dewey's view, see, e.g., his *How We Think* (Boston: D. C. Heath, 1933); for Conant's view see his *On Understanding Science* (New Haven: Yale University Press, 1947) and his *Science and Common Sense* (New Haven: Yale University Press, 1951); for Schwab's view, see Joseph J. Schwab, 'The Nature of Scientific Knowledge as Related to Liberal Education,' *Journal of General Education*, 3 (1949), pp. 245–66, and also his *Science, Curriculum, and Liberal Education: Selected Essays*, ed. by Ian Westbury and Neil J. Wilkof (University of Chicago Press, 1978).
31 Max Wertheimer, *Productive Thinking* (New York: Harper, 1945 [enlarged edition, 1959]).
32 G. Polya, *How to Solve It*, 2nd edition (Garden City: Doubleday, 1957).
33 D. N. Perkins, *The Mind's Best Work* (Cambridge, Mass.: Harvard University Press, 1981).
34 Alan H. Schoenfeld, 'Presenting a Strategy for Indefinite Integration,' *Amer. Mathematical Monthly*, 85 (8) (1978), pp. 673–8; Schoenfeld, 'Can Heuristics Be Taught?' in Jack Lochhead and John Clement, eds, *Cognitive Process Instruction* (Philadelphia: Franklin Institute, 1979); and Schoenfeld, 'Explicit Heuristic Training as a Variable in Problem Solving Performance,' *Journal for Research in Mathematics Education*, 10 (3) (1979), pp. 173–87.
35 Perkins, op. cit., pp. 196–7.
36 Ibid., p. 213.
37 Rogers, Colletta and Mbindyo, op. cit., pp. 271–2.
38 John Dewey, *Democracy and Education* (New York: Macmillan, 1916; Macmillan Paperbacks edition, 1961), pp. 88–91.
39 Ibid., p 252.
40 John Dewey, 'Democracy and Educational Administration' (an

address to the National Education Association, 1937), *School and Society*, 45 (3 April 1937), pp. 457–62. Cited passage reprinted in Joseph Ratner, ed., *Intelligence in the Modern World: John Dewey's Philosophy* (New York: Modern Library, 1939), pp. 403–4.
41 David Perkins, 'Constructive Learning', unpublished manuscript, 12 March 1984.
42 *A Nation at Risk*, a report of the National Commission on Excellence in Education (Washington, DC, 26 April 1983), p. 13.
43 *Educating Americans for the 21st Century*, a report of the National Science Board Commission on Precollege Education in Mathematics, Science and Technology (Washington, DC, 12 September 1983), p. vii.
44 Ibid., pp. 12–13.
45 Ibid., p. 14.

CHAPTER IV THE EDUCATION OF POLICY-MAKERS

1 On related points, see Joseph J. Schwab, *Science, Curriculum, and Liberal Education*, ed. Ian Westbury and Neil J. Wilkof (University of Chicago Press, 1978). For critical discussion of some of Schwab's views, see ch. 16 of my *Reason and Teaching* (Indianapolis: Bobbs-Merrill, 1973).
2 See ibid., pp. 54–6.
3 For discussion of this theme in connection with the teacher's role, ibid., ch. 5.
4 See above, Chapter I, note 10.
5 F. A. Olafson, *The Dialectic of Action* (University of Chicago Press, 1979), p. 140.
6 See above, Chapter I, note 20.
7 The discussion of the next several paragraphs draws upon my 'Moral Education and the Democratic Ideal,' in *Reason and Teaching*, pp. 136–45.
8 Ralph Barton Perry, *Realms of Value* (Cambridge, Mass.: Harvard University Press, 1954), pp. 431–2.
9 Ibid.
10 For a penetrating discussion of this theme, see Olafson, op. cit., pp. 233–61.

INDEX

action, 17–19, 22–4, 26–7, 30–4, 36, 38, 40, 116; consequences of, 17, 22, 31–3; explanatory model for, 19; and policy, 117–18
agency, 22–3, 29, 39, 58, 64–5, 82–4, 98, 105, 116–18
algorithm, 87
amblyopia, 73
anthropology, 3–4
Aquinas, 131n5
Aristotle, 26, 42–4, 92–3, 130n17, 131n1–n4
arts, 28
Augustine, 131n5
autonomy, 35, 39
auxiliary conditions, 75–6, 106–7

Bacon, Francis, 87, 134n29
Baier, Kurt, 130n18
basic skills, 70, 85–91, 95
Beck, Lewis White, 129n14, 130n29, n32
belief, 18–19, 21–2, 49, 65
belief-purpose schema, 102
belief system, 66
benevolence, 82
biology, *see* preventive biological factors

canalization, 70, 77–9, 85
capability, 45, 58–63, 65–6, 70, 83–4, 91; to become, 58ff, 85; and choice, 82–91, 122; and conditional prediction, 58, 60–1, 83; enhancing, 59, 62, 84, 90; to learn or acquire, 84–7, 89; notion of potential, 70, 82–3, 86; self-determining, 84, 89–90, 121; and skill, 58, 61; and valuation, 61–2
capacity, 45–51, 59–60, 62, 64, 70; to acquire, 47, 53, 64; and capability contrasted, 90; as denial of preventive circumstances, 47–9, 51; *see also* preventive circumstances; enhancing, 59; to learn, 12; manifest, 47; as possibility, 47; and prevention, 70–6
Cassirer, Ernst, 128n7
categorical imperative, 36–7
central tendencies in development, 70
child, 10, 27–9, 41–2, 44, 50, 66, 74, 78, 85, 104–8, 111–12, 129n12
choice, 7, 15, 17, 23, 26, 28, 30, 32–3, 37, 59–62, 65–6, 82–92, 95, 104, 118; *see also* decision
claim, concept of, 124
Clarke, A. M. and A. D. B., 74–5, 133n11
cognitive-developmental view, 86
Cohen, Morris R., 134n25, n29
community, 23, 27, 29, 65, 116–17
community self-help, 90–1

Index

Conant, James, 88, 134n30

conditional prediction, 52, 54–8, 64, 76–7, 80, 82–3; *see also* propensity, as conditional prediction

continuity, 110–13

critical periods, 13, 70, 72–6, 86

critical powers, 124

cross-cultural study, 40, 75–6, 106

cultural relativism, 39

culture, 23, 29–30, 38–9, 89, 105–7, 117–18

curriculum, 94–5, 113; design, 86; for educational decision-makers, 7, 99; as metaphor, 99

decision, 4, 28–9, 33, 58–61, 113–14, 116–18, 120, *see also* choice; to learn, 86; of principle, 28, 116; social constraints on, 90

decision-making, 2, 3, 6, 90

deductivism, 87

democracy, 93, 97, 122–5

demythologizing potential, 92–7

Descartes, 87, 131n5

desirability, 31, 35

desire, 26–8, 31–4

development, 56, 64–5, 72, 74, 76–82, 90, 103, 131n2; from and to, 77; internalization of, 83; international, 70, 79–82, 90; as a metaphor, 78; and sequential chains, 54, 56–8, 77–8, 111; and value, 56–7

developmentalism, 111

Dewey, John, 28, 31–2, 85, 88, 92–3, 95, 128n3, n8, 129n13, 130n19, n24–n26, 131n2, 134n27, n30, n38–n40

Dews, P. B., 132n3

dignity, 38–9, 85, 103, 121, 125

disciplinary inquiry, 35, 100

disciplines: and educational practice, 127n4; integration of, 4, 100

Discourse on Method, 87

discovery method, 87

disvalues, 15

domino theory of prediction, 55, 77, 83

Dore, Ronald, 134n24

Dray, William, 132n9

Easley, J. A., Jr., 134n30

education, 25–8, 44, 62, 123–4; aims of, 25, 28, 84; democratic vs. non-democratic, 124; as development, 56; of policy makers, Chap. IV (98–126) *see also* policy; as a profession, 5; and temporal continuity, 113

educational decision, 35, 39

educational metaphors, 78

educational outcomes, 78–9

educational policy, *see* policy, educational

educational planning, 14

educational practice, 3–4, 34, 94, 113

educational responsibility, 11, 14–15

educational theory, *see* theory of education

effort, 58–60, 64

emotion, 30–3; moral, 32

empirical applications (of the theory of potential), 68ff

empowering, 59–62, 65, 83–5, 121

enabling, 60, 65

ends: kingdom of, 39, 124; persons as, 37–8, 85

ends-means continuum, 31

environment, 78; concept of, 21; normative, 116, 118

equal treatment, 37

equality, 39

essence, 7, 42, 44, 47, 49, 63; value implications, 43, 45, 104

essentialism, 45, 77, 92, 106, 118, 131n3

ethical claim, 26–7, 35

ethical point of view, 7, 98

experience, early, 73–4, 116

explanation, 27; *see also* teleological explanation

fear, 30–3, 38

foresight, 12, 30–3

Frankena, William K., 130n17–n18, n28

free will, 59

137